Mary Jane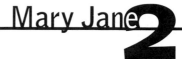

a novel by
Judith O'Brien

with illustrations by
Mike Mayhew

Marvel Entertainment Group, Inc.

First Edition

MARY JANE 2. First printing 2004. ISBN# 0-7851-1433-5. Published by MARVEL COMICS, a division of
MARVEL ENTERTAINMENT GROUP, INC. OFFICE OF PUBLICATION: 10 East 40th Street, New York, NY
10016. Copyright © 2004 Marvel Characters, Inc. All rights reserved. $14.99 per copy in the U.S. and $24.00 in
Canada (GST #R127032852); Canadian Agreement #40668537. All characters featured in this publication and the
distinctive names and likenesses thereof, and all related indicia are trademarks of Marvel Characters, Inc.

ALLEN LIPSON, Chief Executive Officer and General Counsel; AVI ARAD, Chief Creative Officer; GUI KARYO,
President of Publishing and CIO; JOE QUESADA, Editor in Chief; DAN BUCKLEY, Publisher; DAVID BOGART,
Managing Editor; DAVID GABRIEL, Manager - Sales Administration; JEFF YOUNGQUIST, Special Projects
Manager; TOM MARVELLI, Creative Director; JENNIFER LEE, Editor; MEGHAN KERNS, Book Designer;
RUWAN JAYATILLEKE, Proofreader; STAN LEE, Chairman Emeritus.

For information regarding advertising in Marvel Comics or on Marvel.com, please contact Russell Brown, Executive
Vice President, Consumer Products, Promotions and Media Sales at rbrown@marvel.com or 212-576-8561.

Library of Congress Control Number 2003113544

10 9 8 7 6 5 4 3 2 1

For Seth

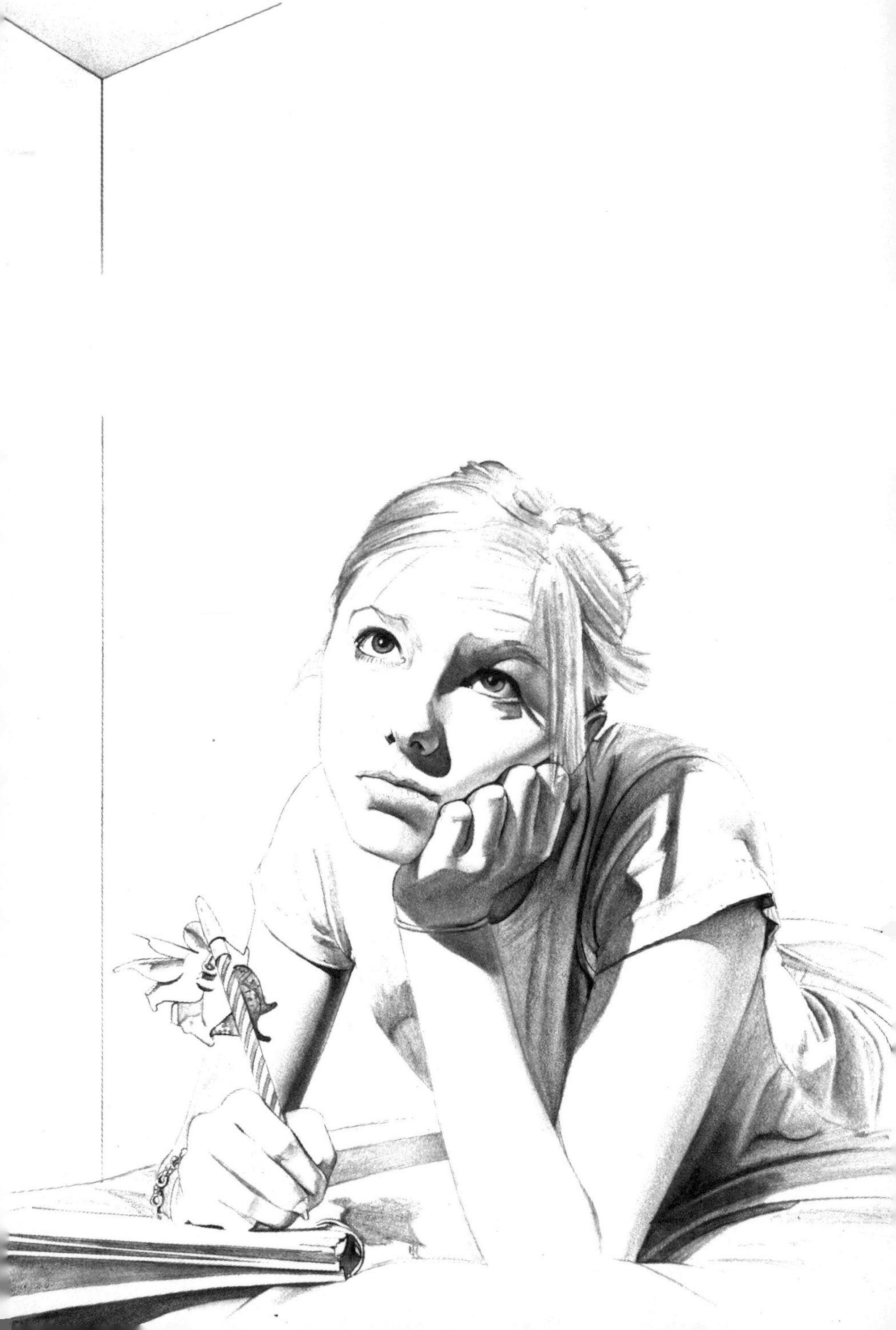

chapter 1

Two lone figures sat huddled shoulder to shoulder on the bleachers of Midtown High School's football field. The chill November wind whipped the afternoon air, sending autumn's last leaves swirling over the grass. In the distance, the spectral skyscrapers of Manhattan glowed against the graying horizon, their lights flickering and dancing. It seemed a million miles from the field and the teenage girls in Queens watching the boys' varsity soccer practice.

"Tell me again why we're here," Mary Jane Watson said between gritted teeth, rubbing her hands together. "I'm freezing."

Wendy Gonzales didn't take her eyes off the field. "We're here because that guy I like is on the soccer team, and I want to get a good look at him."

"Can't we wait until spring to check him out?" Mary Jane closed her eyes against a sudden frigid bluster, her nose slightly red from the cold, then opened them again, squinting as the bits of dried leaves blew past. But even frozen and red-nosed, Mary Jane was lovely, with delicate features that contrasted against the stubborn set of her chin. She reached up and pushed a thatch of auburn hair from her face. "By May he'll even be wearing shorts *off* the soccer field."

"By May, I may not be interested in him. Gotta see him now." With that Wendy opened her backpack and fished around for a few moments, producing the pen she'd been looking for in first period. "Ah-ha," she announced in

1

triumph. Raising her dark eyebrows at Mary Jane, she pulled out what looked like an ornate set of miniature binoculars.

"You've got to be joking. Binoculars?"

"Please, my dear. Nothing so boring as binoculars. I'll have you know these are genuine opera glasses. Antique, or at least old. They belong to my Aunt Vanessa," Wendy shrugged. "She's crazy about the opera and ballet. All Broadway shows. Stadium rock shows. College lectures in big halls. Actually, she's just plain crazy, but let's not get into that." She held the handle tightly and flicked the lenses over, then peered through them for a moment. "Whoops, Kevin McBride missed a header. Ouch. He hit the post instead. And Martin Wolf has red leg hair. Hmm, where's my guy?"

Wendy scanned the field like an eagle, then brightened. "There he is. Wow! Check him out!"

"Opera glasses are just fancy binoculars. Let me see." Mary Jane grasped at the opera glasses, but Wendy held them just beyond her reach.

"Wait a minute! You *have* a boyfriend. My turn to have a little fun for a change." A slow grin spread across Wendy's face as she returned to her viewing. "Hello, cute boy!"

"Which one is he?"

"Blue sweatshirt, dribbling on the sidelines."

"Dribbling, or drooling? I can't see a thing from here. And they all have blue sweatshirts."

"I'm the one doing the drooling at the moment, thank you very much. He's just dribbling. Wow, look at him go! He sure has nice..."

"Nice what? Come on, let me see!"

They nudged each other for a few moments, giggling as they engaged in a mock battle for the opera glasses.

"Hello, girls," came a masculine voice out of nowhere.

Both Wendy and Mary Jane shrieked as they jumped, the opera glasses tumbling to the ground beneath the bleachers along with Mary Jane's backpack.

"Peter!" Mary Jane was the first to recover. "You scared us half to death!"

Peter Parker's handsome, yet somehow not extraordinary, face dissolved into a slow grin. "A little extracurricular stalking, ladies?"

"Dude," Wendy groaned. "Not cool. Those are my aunt's opera glasses."

"*Oprah* glasses? Specially designed for daytime talk show watching?" But as he spoke he swung gracefully to the ground, scooped up the glasses and MJ's backpack, and returned easily to the seats. He examined the opera glasses, then peered through them at the soccer practice. "Who am I looking for?"

Mary Jane smiled at him, her boyfriend. Her actual, undeniable boyfriend. The thought of having a boyfriend still made her feel peculiar, but in a very satisfied way. A warmth spread through her as she watched his profile, a gust of wind teasing his hair.

They had known each other forever, since they were little kids. It had been only recently that things changed between them, that solid friendship had given way to deep romance. But wow, what a change. She took a sharp breath, hoping this fullness would stay within her every time she saw him.

And she knew he felt the same way about her. As confusing as the past few months had been, especially after the death of his Uncle Ben, the one thing Mary Jane knew for certain was their feelings for each other. She watched his features, his face just inches from hers. Even the mere thought of how he grieved the night of his uncle's murder, sobbing heavily in her arms, made her blink back tears, if she wasn't careful. That experience had given him a reluctant maturity beyond his years, a depth of soul that was evident every time she looked into his eyes. There was a new compassion there, an empathy that was touching in its sincerity and breadth.

"Gross," he exclaimed. "Martin Wolf has red leg hair!" He elbowed Wendy. "Is that your new main man?"

"Get outta here!" Wendy pushed him back. "Please. Give me some credit. I'm not at all interested in the Big Bad Red Wolf." Then her voice took on an air of mystery. "I don't think I'm going to tell you guys who it is."

"Come on," MJ groaned. "You dragged me out here in the freezing cold..."

"Actually, it's only about fifty-five," Peter offered helpfully.

"When did you become the weatherman?" Mary Jane gave him a playful shove. "Wendy, give it up."

"Yeah, Wendy." He kept his hold on the glasses. "Are you sure it's not someone from the football team?" They were practicing on the other end of the field.

"No way," Wendy shook her head, her dark curls bouncing. "I hate football. You can't see their faces or their build. Soccer gives you all that and more."

"Yeah, red leg hair," mumbled Peter.

"How about basketball?" Mary Jane leaned against Peter. Until recently, he had been the sudden and unexpected star of the varsity basketball team. Out of nowhere, it seemed, he went from geek to Greek god, showing an amazing athletic ability, shooting three-pointers every game and running circles around the opponents as well as his own teammates. But Uncle Ben's death had changed all that. He no longer had the time, nor the inclination, for the long daily practices and weekend games. He was completely devoted to Uncle Ben's widow, Aunt May.

"Basketball?" Wendy wrinkled her nose. "Sorry, Peter, but basketball is a little too up close and personal for my taste. All that grunting and sweating, not to mention the weird squeaking sounds the shoes make on the court. Nope, give me soccer any day."

Peter turned to Wendy and watched the direction of her eyes. He followed her line of vision, then smiled. "Dave Lipinski."

Wendy gasped. "How did you know?"

"Just a guess. He's a nice guy. Not particularly bright, but a nice enough guy."

"Who needs bright? It's overrated." Then Wendy looked at both Peter and MJ. "Think I can get him to ask me to the Winter Formal?"

"Sure, why not?" Peter stood up abruptly. "I've got to go. Aunt May needs me to fix the faucet in the kitchen. Uncle Ben used to take care of all that stuff, but, well. Now it's up to me." Without pausing he pulled off his gray Midtown High sweatshirt, revealing surprisingly buff arms and torso in a tee shirt. "Here," he leaned towards Mary Jane. "Arms up."

"I really don't need..." she began.

"Please?" He cocked his head slightly, and Mary Jane felt that wonderful warm rush again. She smiled and allowed him to slip his sweatshirt on her, still hot from his body. It smelled of him, too, of soap and something else that was just

Peter. "Later," he said to both girls, before glancing one last time at Mary Jane.

"Okay," she said, her voice a mere peep.

And then he was off, stepping down the bleachers and jogging off the field.

"Wow," said Wendy. "He's really nuts about you. Did you see the look in his eyes?"

"Sort of. I mean, it still feels a little weird to see him without glasses." Much less to be his girlfriend, was the unspoken end to that sentence.

"If Dave Lipinski ever looked at me like that, I think I'd pass out."

"That would impress him." MJ watched as Peter faded from sight.

"Hey, speaking of impressing people — did you hear the school musical auditions are in a few days?"

"Really? What musical are they doing?"

"My *Fair Lady*. Cool, eh? I love that show."

"Yep," she agreed, wondering what time Peter would call her that evening. He knew she had ballet class, so probably after ten, but not too late. He was always really considerate of that, knowing her mother worked and had to get up early and...

Wendy had stopped speaking. Then she rolled her eyes. "You did hear me, didn't you? Or were you zoning out again?"

Mary Jane flushed slightly. "Of course I heard you."

"So will you?"

With only a brief hesitation, she nodded. "Sure I will."

"Great! This will be so fun! What if we both make it into the cast? Wouldn't that be cool?"

MJ blinked a few times before realizing she had just agreed to try out for the school musical.

"Oh, well," she thought to herself. "How bad could it be?"

* * *

Three days later she had the answer: Pretty bad.

There she was, backstage at the school's auditorium, after having just mangled "Wouldn't It be Lover-ly?" and waiting for Wendy's turn to go next. Why had that same song sounded so great in the shower a mere six hours earlier? And Mary Jane's mom had even helped her with stage makeup tips, employing her skills as a former contestant in the Miss Tennessee pageant.

"Here, hon," her mother said as she added more eyeliner and shadow to MJ's face. "This way your eyes will pop right out."

The image of her eyes rolling to the foot of the stage hadn't been particularly welcome until she began her audition song. That's when her voice cracked, and she stubbed her toe on a music stand during the second verse. The piano player had to stop a few lines later, accusing her of changing keys in the middle of the song.

Keys? She was singing in keys?

At least she did well in the dancing part of the audition, which was actually fun. She had tons of experience dancing in front of an audience through ballet. In fact, she could tell the director really liked what she could do. He even asked her to perform a few extra steps, which she embellished with a high kick or two.

But poor Wendy had never been on a stage before, and it showed.

"I don't know if I can do this," she hissed to MJ as the person before her was just finishing up.

"You did much better than Becky," MJ soothed.

"Becky's in a neck brace! And at least she didn't dance into the orchestra pit!"

"Hey, you only came close. You never actually took a full dive. And you have a great voice."

"I do?" Wendy was like a drowning man grasping for anything that would float.

"Totally. I've heard you sing along with the radio. You're fantastic." MJ hoped she sounded completely sincere, since in fact she had only heard Wendy sing brief snatches of songs. It was impossible to tell if she was any good.

Wendy shot MJ a panicked glare. "Promise me you'll do the play with me if we both get in."

"Wendy, did you see me? I was awful, I doubt I'll..."

"Just promise me." She grabbed MJ's hand. "Come on, I can't do this alone."

"Wendy Gonzales?" Mr. Toby, the director, called out. "Are you here, Wendy Gonzales?"

Wendy stared at MJ, silently pleading.

"Okay, I promise," MJ said. "*If* I get in."

"Last call for Wendy Gonzales..."

Mary Jane smiled and squeezed her best friend's hand. "Just go out there and break a leg."

"I almost did that before," she moaned as she walked out to the center of the stage. "Now I'm just going to puke."

Mary Jane thought she, too, would throw up. She closed her eyes and began a silent prayer. The piano player began the opening chords of "I Could Have Danced All Night."

Please, please, let her do well! Please, please, please....

And then Mary Jane heard something amazing. She opened her eyes at the first note, and then her jaw dropped.

It was the song all right. And there was Wendy, standing center stage, her hands clasped tightly in front of her. Her mouth was moving.

And her voice was really good! Better than that. It was clear and pure, and seemed, at least to Mary Jane's ears, completely on key.

It was almost like one of those old cornball Hollywood movies, where the shy kid is pushed to perform, and morphs into a star. Wendy wasn't quite a star, but she sounded every bit as good as Linda De Marco did, and Linda was always bragging about taking voice lessons and going on auditions.

All the background noise dropped out as everyone else in the auditorium stopped whatever they were doing to listen to Wendy. A few smiled. The custodian stopped his sweeping. It was just so unexpected to see a normal kid, not one of those freaky theater kids, get up on stage and really do well.

Wendy glanced at Mary Jane, who smiled broadly at her as she continued the song. Now she added a little movement as her confidence grew, walking across the stage, singing to the director, who had stood up in the audience and walked to the lip of the stage. He, too, seemed both surprised and delighted. And at the end she managed to hold the note, even trilling up a notch on the final syllable.

There was slight pause, and then Mr. Toby said "Excellent, Miss Gonzales. Excellent!"

Everyone applauded, which was amazing. When all the other kids auditioned, people just clapped politely once or twice. Or worse, they cleared their throats and looked away.

"Did you hear that?"

"She was fantastic!"

Suddenly Wendy was surrounded by people. Everyone was grabbing her hand or patting her back. The piano player just sat on the bench, smiling happily as he straightened his music.

"Was I really okay?" Wendy asked earnestly the moment she was able to get close enough to Mary Jane.

It took MJ a second to realize she was serious. She really wasn't sure.

"Oh, Wendy." Mary Jane let her laughter erupt. "You were seriously amazing!"

Only then did Wendy take a deep breath, give Mary Jane an ear-to-ear grin, and start talking to her new fans.

In the flurry of activity, the director huddled with several other faculty members. And within fifteen minutes, the cast list was posted. Wendy was Eliza, the lead. And Mary Jane was a member of the chorus.

Mary Jane backed away slightly, excited about the musical, and even more thrilled to see her friend embraced by everyone. But also, a strange thought went through her mind, almost a premonition: Maybe, just maybe, this would change everything.

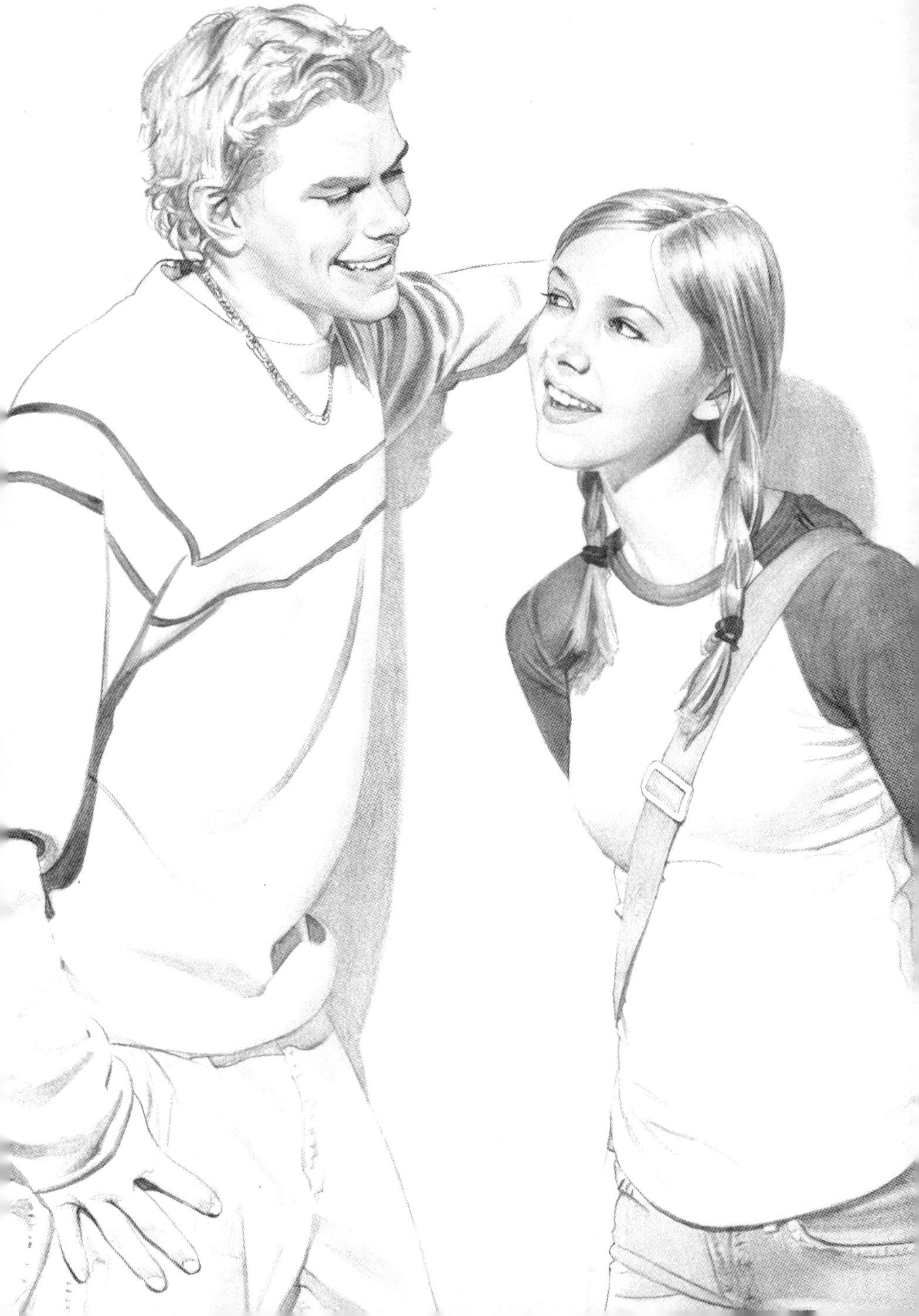

chapter 2

"Hey, MJ," called Harry Osborn, one of Midtown High's best looking guys, from across the front steps of the school. The bell ringing the end of eighth period blasted, and he shrugged and paused until the noise stopped reverberating. "A bunch of us are going-to see the new zombie flick over at the Pavilion. Scored half price tickets online. Want to come?"

Her immediate reaction was yes, absolutely! After all, she hadn't seen much of Harry recently. He'd been laying low since his dad, Norman Osborn, was marched off to a maximum-security prison upstate for illegally testing his company's drug-enhanced sports drink at school. Harry had his hands full just trying to adjust from being Midtown's resident rich kid to being eligible for the dreaded free hot lunch in the cafeteria. The mansion he and his dad had lived in was seized by the state, so now he was living with an aunt in a little flat in Brooklyn. This new financial status was only temporary, since his dad's lawyers were getting him early access to his trust fund money. But for now, the golden boy, whose biggest decision of the day used to be which sports car to drive, rode the subway (or even worse, the bus).

The change had been a definite shock not only to Harry, but also to the whole high school. He was still great looking, with model-like features under carefully styled hair. But the near-mystical aura of self-confidence was gone, along with all the cool kids who used to hang around him. There were no longer cheerleaders hanging on his arm, or the school's star athletes asking if they can have a homecoming party at the Osborn estate. Unlike most kids, he'd never had to try to make friends before. They always came to him. Until now.

Mary Jane looked at the gang behind him, mostly freshmen guys who were clustered together. Something about them set off her inner radar. Maybe it was the way they were looking her up and down. She couldn't explain it exactly; she just had a bad feeling about them. Then the short kid in the oversized army surplus jacket actually sneered at her. What a creep.

Harry stood alone on a lower step.

Mary Jane sighed to herself and walked towards him. As she got closer she tried to smile with genuine warmth. "I'd love to go, Harry. But I've got ballet class."

"Oh." He seemed a little crestfallen. "I get it."

"No, really. It's a total drag. I really want to see this one. I hear there's a completely disgusting scene with an electric knife and a sheriff, or a deputy. Something like that."

He brightened slightly. "A traffic cop."

"Yeah!" She couldn't believe she'd had a major crush on him earlier in the year. It lasted about twenty minutes, until he got a little *too* friendly, but still. And her switch to Peter had nothing to do with the Norman Osborn scandal, but since it all happened around the same time, she worried that was exactly what Harry thought. That she lost interest in him when he lost the right to live in that big house, or to take an afternoon spin in a bright yellow Porsche.

"Hey, maybe this weekend?" Mary Jane offered, working up enthusiasm. "You and me and Peter can do something. I don't have ballet Saturday afternoon, and I think Peter's free. That would be great, wouldn't it?"

"Maybe." Then he turned to the other kids. "Does anyone know which bus we take to the Pavilion?"

And then he was off with his new gang.

Mary Jane watched him leave, towering over his new friends, laughing self-consciously at something no one else was laughing at.

Really, he wasn't such a bad guy. He was just a victim of his own father, along with every other kid at Midtown who had been used as an unwitting guinea pig for Osborn Industries. But that was all in the past. Life had gone on, the saga of Norman Osborn and his over-the-top criminal greed was no longer relevant. For everyone, that is, except Harry.

And for Mary Jane and Peter. It was they who first discovered the criminal activities led by Harry's father. Osborn Industries was literally poisoning thousands of kids, a few of whom were still hospitalized. Once they got hard evidence, they tipped off the police anonymously.

And although they rarely mentioned it to each other, they were both filled with guilt for what had happened to their friend Harry. The emotional fallout had been every bit as devastating as the financial consequences. They'd had no choice but to turn in Norman Osborn, but that indisputable truth didn't make Harry's fate any easier to accept. No matter how much Mary Jane reassured herself that they did the right thing, she couldn't quite believe it one hundred percent. So she tried instead to focus on being a good friend to him now.

Peter had tried to reach out to Harry as much as possible, too. Yesterday he had told MJ about a conversation they'd had the previous week.

"I feel as if every day is a red-letter day now," Harry had confided to Peter, pointing at his own chest. "You know what I mean."

Peter had nodded somberly as if he knew exactly what Harry meant. "Sure I do."

A red-letter day?

Harry continued. "Just like that Hester chick with the baby. You know, in pilgrim times."

That's when it had dawned on Peter: *The Scarlet Letter* by Nathaniel Hawthorne. Of course Harry wouldn't know the finer points of classic American literature. Up until a few weeks ago, Peter himself had been doing most of Harry's homework for him, including last year's paper on Hawthorne. Actually, it was impressive he even recalled that the main character had been visually marked as an outcast in her community.

Peter had awkwardly patted Harry's back. "I know exactly what you mean, buddy."

So that's how it was with Harry now. He felt marked, forever branded, even if only Harry himself saw the brand. Mary Jane sighed and made a mental note to talk to Peter later about taking him out this weekend.

That is, if Peter was back from his new mission. For at that precise moment, he was attempting to peddle some of his amateur photographs of the afternoon football game against Tech to the *Daily Bugle*. In so doing, he could forever call himself a professional photographer. And to Peter, that was a very big deal.

Not only would that make him a real photographer, but he would get some extra cash as well. That was something the Parker household needed. Badly.

16

The pictures were good, really good, she had to admit. He'd been working on the school paper for a while now, but only recently had he developed a new confidence in his abilities, a sudden sense that he could do much more than just be the nerd.

His photographs reflected a genuine artistry, a real gift for capturing a fleeting moment at the height of dramatic tension. One of his pictures was of the injured Tech quarterback watching from the sidelines as Midtown scored the pivotal touchdown. It was a moving portrait of disappointment and loss, of a young kid caught up in the moment. And at that precise instant, the game was everything to the boy, and that all-consuming emotion was reflected in the expression on his face, his mouth slightly open, his helmet clutched to his side. The photo stood alone as a summary of the last plays of the game.

That was interesting enough. What was really fascinating was how he also managed to capture the winning touchdown at almost the exact same second! The other picture was of Midtown's player, his foot just touching the dusty chalk line, his own expression one of jubilation, his eyes partially closed in a perfect reflection of sublime triumph. Just behind him, also in crystal-clear focus, was a Tech tackle, his arms reaching out but grasping nothing but air and frustration, feet tangled across each other just as he was about to slam into the turf.

Both photos were bold and technically impressive, in moody black and white. To Mary Jane, however, who had known Peter since their early days at an elite private grade school, the most remarkable aspect of those pictures was not the finished product, but the photographer himself. This was a new Peter, someone just exploring the possibilities life had to offer. Someone trying out a previously unknown talent. She wondered how many other talents were waiting to bloom.

It was something much deeper than losing those thick glasses he used to wear, or getting the first non-bowl haircut he'd had since third grade. Wendy thought it was Mary Jane herself who had given him a boost when so much else in his life, mainly his uncle's murder, should have sent him into a total tailspin. But as pleased as she was with Wendy's assessment, Mary Jane knew she couldn't take full credit, or even most of the credit.

No, that belonged to Peter himself.

She swung her backpack over her shoulder as she passed through the subway turnstile on her way to ballet.

At that moment, as Peter was no doubt pestering the staff of the *Bugle*, she knew Wendy was front and center in play rehearsals. She could have gone with Peter to the newspaper, just as she could have been watching Wendy in practice, even though the chorus wasn't needed until Monday.

She also could have gone to the movie with Harry, and maybe offered him a little much-needed friendship. Or she could have done all of her homework, then watched TV and talked on the phone all night with friends, just like a normal teenager. There were so many things she could have been doing that afternoon.

Instead she was taking three subway trains to the Manhattan School of Ballet. As she waited for her train she looked over the newsstand, the bold-lettered headlines about the Spider-Man, the mysterious new character. Good or evil? No one seemed to know, but the papers were having a swell time guessing.

Her train came, the lights curving around the tracks.

She still found it hard to believe that she was on full scholarship at the Manhattan School of Ballet. Unlike most dancers, even those who could afford to pay dreamed of being offered a scholarship like hers, one based on talent. She'd had a secret patron before, someone who paid her tuition but wished to remain anonymous. After the paid lessons were completed, the MSB had offered her the most prestigious scholarship of all, and she had gladly accepted.

To Mary Jane, ballet was nothing short of magic. Everything about it was amazing, from the long hours it took to practice and perfect each move, to the thrill of a recital or performance, and everything in-between.

For a while she was taking lessons six days a week. And at first that had been amazing, all she had ever wanted. Then came Peter, who fully supported her dreams of becoming a professional dancer.

But the scholarship also meant sacrifice, including sacrificing time with Peter. And Wendy. Some weeks she found herself losing track of time and realizing all too late that she had accidently skipped a class. Not really, though. She was saying that to herself, to justify why she was still hanging around in Queens well after her five o'clock Advanced II class had begun.

She climbed the steps out of the subway station, wondering how she was going to explain to her teachers, especially the great Yuri Ivanovich, that she would only be at lessons three days a week until the school musical was over.

The Manhattan School of Ballet building loomed ahead as always, impressive in its sleek lines and the shiny brass "MSB" under the much larger "MBT" sign, for the

Manhattan Ballet Theater. A sense of excitement and wonder always tingled through her at that first glimpse of the building. She had arrived, both physically and figuratively. Once she entered those glass doors, she would be the class pet, asked to demonstrate steps as an example to the others.

"Very nice, Mary Jane," an instructor would say in whatever accent, authentic or faked. "Class, look at her turn-out. See her thighs, almost flat? Her knees over her toes, no rolling in?"

She had good feet, a decent extension, graceful hands — and less enthusiasm than she'd had even the week before.

What was wrong with her?

Almost automatically, she went upstairs to the studio, signed in with Nadia at the front desk. She slipped into the dressing room and changed into her MSB regulation pink tights and shoes, and black leotard. Hair in a neat bun. Off the eyes. No chewing gum or excessive makeup; save the paint for the stage.

Recently she'd been noticing new things about ballet, about the studio itself. It always smelled musty and dank, no matter what season, no matter what the temperature was outside. It was a moist heat, of thermostats turned way up to keep the muscles loose. Of overheated bodies clad in layers of wool warm-up clothes before class, perspiration clashing with this morning's perfume.

The floor was wooden and discolored in places. In the corner was a little bucket of white powder rosin to keep the satin toe shoes from slipping. The dancers would wait their turn to dip their feet into the bucket, talking about who was dancing in what ballet, how a Russian ballerina was fired for gaining too much weight. Sometimes they would chat about a sale at the leotard store, or about how someone had cut their hair too short and now it was hard to put back into a bun. And above all, there was always talk about food and diets, about some miracle pill or powder or shake guaranteed to make the pounds melt away.

Mary Jane stayed out of those conversations. Her own dangerous experiment with dieting, or rather, not eating, was still too fresh. And her reluctance to join in the chatter was noticed by the other girls.

The pianist arrived and took his place, poised and ready to begin. And finally, after waiting for the entire class to line up at the *barre*, the instructor entered. Today it was Elaina, who had been a soloist with the Manhattan Ballet Theater until about five years earlier, when she had been unceremoniously asked to retire.

"That's the problem with being a principle or a soloist," she had once admitted to Mary Jane. "They can't move you back to the corps, because the corps is already filled with the eager young dancers who may be the next big thing. So they ask you to go away, to teach someplace or to join a lesser company."

The class was a good one, and once again Mary Jane was singled out for her elbows in second position, and her arches *en pointe*.

But after class Elaina asked to see her.

"Is there anything wrong, Mary Jane?"

"What do you mean?"

"You just seem distracted, a bit off. It's as if your body's here dancing, and your mind is somewhere else." Elaina had a towel around her neck and was dabbing her own face.

The studio was always hot as a rain forest after the ninety-minute advanced class. And it always smelled like feet.

"No, I'm okay," Mary Jane began. Then she hesitated.

Elaina smiled, "Out with it, Watson. You can tell me."

She might as well get it over with. "Well, I. You see, I have a part in the school musical."

Elaina's expression was blank.

"High School. Midtown. We're doing *My Fair Lady*."

"So?"

"Well, once practice for the musical begins, I'll have to miss some classes."

"How many classes?"

"I'm not sure. A couple a week, I guess."

Elaina took a deep breath. "A couple a week on top of the classes you've already been missing?"

"I guess so."

Elaina's green eyes narrowed. "You *do* know there are plenty of other girls who would give their front teeth for your position?"

This was harder than she thought. "I realize that. And I'm grateful, truly grateful, for this scholarship." She thought of her promise to Wendy, who was a better friend to her than all the girls at ballet combined. "But can't I occasionally do something else besides ballet?"

"No."

Mary Jane blinked. At first she thought Elaina was just kidding, but very soon realized she was utterly serious. "Excuse me?"

"Listen, Mary Jane. This is no longer an extracurricular activity for you, not at this level. And not with the commitment the MSB has already shown you through the scholarship, as well as through the roles you've been allowed to dance in our showcases."

"Allowed?" Mary Jane swallowed and counted to three, hoping to get control of her temper. Other girls had paused on their way out the door, and were watching with undisguised curiosity. Amanda Peterson and another girl whispered to each other urgently. Was it her imagination, or was Amanda smirking?

Mary Jane lowered her voice. "Elaina, I've worked hard for every part, for every single step I've ever danced or choreographed. And I know with absolute certainty that if I hadn't been good enough, I never would have been allowed to perform. I probably never would have been allowed into this studio.

"Yes, I appreciate what this school has done for me," she continued. "But I've put a lot of myself into everything I've done here."

"But now your interests are divided." Elaina's voice was flat, but not unkind.

"No! I...." She thought for a moment. "Yes, I suppose my interests are a little divided."

Funny. She hadn't really thought of it that way before.

"Believe it or not, I understand. I remember what it was like, not so very long ago." Finally she allowed a small smile. "Hey, I went to high school, too. Granted, I didn't graduate. But I did go to high school for almost two years."

"You never graduated from high school?"

"Of course not. At sixteen I was invited to join the company, and there wasn't any time to finish high school. To have a boyfriend. To try out for a school musical. But there comes a time, Mary Jane, when you have to make a decision.

Either ballet will be your career, your entire life, or it won't. It's as simple as that."

"Yeah, but it's not as if I have to decide that right now," Mary Jane shrugged with a light laugh.

Elaina did not join in the laughter. "Yes, it is. That's the problem. With any other career — even other athletic careers — there is time for high school and college. It's even encouraged. There's an off-season. Spring training. Whatever. Not with ballet. You can never slacken off, because if you do you may never get it back." She was now staring hard at Mary Jane.

"There's always someone working harder and longer, who's more hungry for the dance than you are. You get distracted, you get injured. Even if you're not in a performance, you must take classes six days a week, fifty-two weeks a year," she continued. "And then, as a reward, by the time most careers are just beginning, a ballet dancer's is usually just ending."

Mary Jane took a few moments to absorb what was being said. It was nothing new, nothing she hadn't heard a hundred times from a dozen other people. But before when she had heard those words, she had been absolutely certain that this was the life she wanted. This was all she had ever desired: To be a ballerina in the Manhattan Ballet Theater.

Now she wasn't so certain.

She was almost afraid of what she was about to ask. She cleared her throat. "Do you ever regret your choice?"

"Never," Elaina replied without hesitation. "But then," she began, her gaze fixed on Mary Jane.

"But then, what?"

"But then, I never had the courage to even ask that question."

Before Mary Jane could respond, Elaina gave her arm a quick squeeze and left the studio.

Mary Jane watched her as she walked to the main waiting room, from where the dancers were always seen through a big, picture-glass window. Where they were always on display, always performing — if only for parents or other dancers awaiting their own class times.

Elaina did not glance back at her.

Yet Mary Jane thought had seen something in her eyes, a brief, flitting sadness. Or a sense of doubt. Perhaps she had imagined it. But no matter what, she knew that expression would haunt her for a very long time.

* * *

It felt good to be back home.

Mary Jane tossed down her backpack, kicked off her shoes, and looked around the small living room with satisfaction. She remembered so clearly how she had felt about the place when they first moved in, when her Mom had tried to make the best of what had seemed like a hopeless dump.

"It will be great, honey," Madeline Watson had said in her soft Tennessee accent. "You'll see."

She had hated the apartment at first. This address, just off Queens Boulevard, had been the last in a series of increasingly small apartments. Once, a long time ago, they lived in a sprawling Park Avenue duplex, with a uniformed doorman, a big brass elevator that let them out right in their living room, and all of the privileges that went along with being a member of Manhattan's elite. Private schools.

Horseback riding lessons, tennis three times a week. Long dinners at fancy restaurants where nobody ever seemed to care about the bill.

And then her dad left. Not just the apartment, not just New York, but their lives. He simply vanished one day, walked away without bothering to return, and slowly but steadily everything changed. Her mother, who had never held a job in her life, was suddenly forced to work.

It had been hard at first, more difficult than she had ever imagined it could have been. She'd had to leave the Bradford School, the private school where she had first met Peter Parker. Every year, it seemed, she was the new kid in some public school, on the Upper West Side, in Chelsea, in the Village. They even lived in Washington Heights, which was technically still Manhattan but way, *way* uptown. And once they tried out a part of town known as Hell's Kitchen, which made it sound much worse than it actually was. For Mary Jane the hardest part was always fitting in, finding new friends and adjusting to a new school with new cliques and new social rules.

At last they settled in Queens, an outer borough of all places. Mary Jane had been sullen at first, looking at the barren flat and missing where they used to live.

But must to her astonishment, she grew to love it. Of course, it helped to be reunited with her old friend Peter. And she met Wendy. Plus there was the school itself, and all the extra stuff like the musical and having a boyfriend for the very first time.

Even the apartment was looking better. There were small touches, things her mother hadn't bothered with in the other places they had lived. She made bright curtains, and found an area rug on sale that fit perfectly with the rest of the living room.

Her mother had even mentioned the possibility of getting cable TV. Cable! For the first time in years they could get decent reception and MTV! And she also said they could get a better online service for their second-hand computer, not the lame, cheapo one that only allowed them one screen name on the account.

After years of struggling, things were finally coming together. Madeline Watson was proving herself to be an excellent saleswoman for Skye Bleu Cosmetics. Women would see her cool, refined beauty — a throwback to the models and actresses of the fifties — and want to look just like her. Never mind that Madeline Watson had always looked that way, beautiful and remote, no matter how much or how little makeup she wore.

And never mind that many of her new clients were actually friends and acquaintances from their old Park Avenue days, when Madeline was one of the ladies who lunched and Mary Jane was the trophy child. It was rarely mentioned by either makeup salesgal or client.

Yes, it felt good to be home. And she hadn't felt that way in a long time.

Mary Jane smiled as she looked around the place. "Mom?"

"In here, hon," Madeline called from the kitchen.

"Wow, something sure smells good!"

"Roast chicken with rosemary potatoes. And salad. I'm trying out a new vinaigrette from the paper."

It was so great to have a home-cooked meal, to have her mother back with her. For a while it seemed as if every new apartment had brought a new boyfriend for her mom. And each one, Mary Jane thought, was worse than the last one.

"Sounds fantastic. Should I set the table?"

"Sure," and then her mother stepped out from the kitchen, wearing that old calico apron that always cracked Mary Jane up.

She looked at Madeline. There was something decidedly different with her mother. A sparkle in her eye. Something.

Mary Jane's good mood suddenly faded.

"Mom, what's up?" It was impossible to keep the suspicion from her voice.

"Nothing, sweetie pie," her mother replied in a sing-song lilt.

Danger sign. That always meant something was up.

"Are we moving again?"

"Oh, honey, of course not. Why, don't you like it here?"

"Yes, I do. That's why I don't want to move."

"Well then don't you worry your pretty little head! Let's use the good china, shall we?"

The good china! Warning bells were clanging.

"How many places shall I set?"

Her mother smiled graciously. "Two, silly. Just the two of us." Then she practically skipped back into the kitchen, humming.

"Mom, did you have dental work or something today?"

The humming stopped. "Why, am I swollen?"

"No, you're just acting the way you did when Dr. Sangey gave you those pain pills."

Her mother emerged with a picture-perfect, Norman Rockwell-worthy platter of roasted chicken bordered with golden brown potatoes. She was positively beaming.

"Honey, I've met someone. And I think he may be The One," she slid the platter onto the table and skipped back into the kitchen. "Soda, water, or milk?"

Mary Jane stood in the dining room, holding the plates.

Not another guy! Last time her mother had met "The One" it had been an utter disaster. He was an accountant she met in a ballroom dancing class, and he almost had "Madeline Forever" tattooed across the back of his neck.

But Mary Jane kept calm.

"Oh, really?" She placed the plates deliberately on the table. "What does he do?"

What she really meant was, is he in jail? Or, how many times has he been married? Does he wear too much aftershave and make long-distance calls to remote villages in Argentina without asking? Does he...

"I'm not going to say a thing," Madeline Watson pursed her lips. "I'm forgetting something."

"That he wears black socks with sandals and belongs to a cult?"

Her mother didn't bat an eye. "The string beans," she returned to the kitchen.

"Really, Mom. Things are going so well. Please reconsider the beauty and simplicity of single life."

She came back with the beans. "Mary Jane, I have come to the conclusion that it is best for me to get to know someone before I bring him home to meet you."

"Finally!" She must have read all the articles MJ had been leaving around the apartment, the advice columns on how not to traumatize a child by bringing home dates. Of course, the children in question were usually seven. Still, it was good, solid advice.

But now she was curious. "So what's he like?"

Madeline untied her apron. "Let's eat."

"Really, how did you meet him?"

She sat down in her chair. "Could you please pass the salt?"

Mary Jane took her own place with a grin. "You really aren't going to tell me, are you?"

"I'm really not," she winked. "So tell me, how was your day?"

At last Mary Jane relaxed and helped herself to some green beans. "It was fine. Peter showed me some great pictures from the game. And Mom?"

"Yes?" Her mother paused with the pepper mill.

"I'm not sure how I feel about ballet."

Now it was her mother's turn to be surprised. "Do you want to talk about it?"

Mary Jane hesitated just an instant, then she nodded.

And they had a long talk over one of the most delicious meals either had had in a long time.

* * *

"Hey, you," came Peter's voice over the telephone. "Hope I'm not calling too late."

"Nah," Mary Jane's voice was groggy, but she perked up right away. "What time is it?"

"Just after eleven. Sorry, but I only got in a few minutes ago."

"Really? Where were you?"

"Trying to convince the *Daily Bugle* they desperately need my pictures."

"And how did it go?"

"Let's just say they aren't convinced," he chuckled. "Then I went back into the school darkroom to develop another roll. Got a really pretty one of you, by the way."

"Must have been that trick camera lens," she cracked.

"No. It's just a really pretty picture of you. I'm looking at it right now."

"Oh." She didn't know quite what to say.

"And that reminds me, I keep on forgetting to ask you something."

"Yeah?" She twirled the phone cord as she spoke.

"Will you go to the Winter Formal with me?"

Of course she knew he was going to ask her. At least she thought he probably would. Still, it felt wonderful to have him actually ask. She took a deep breath and smiled.

"I'd love to," she said softly.

"Good." She could hear him smile on the other end. Then he paused. "Um, well then. Good night."

"Okay. Sleep well."

"You too," his voice was husky. And then he hung up.

Mary Jane placed the phone back in the receiver. It was too late to call Wendy, but she'd catch her first thing in the morning.

The Winter Formal. She was going to the Winter Formal with Peter Parker.

She fell asleep with that single, wonderful thought.

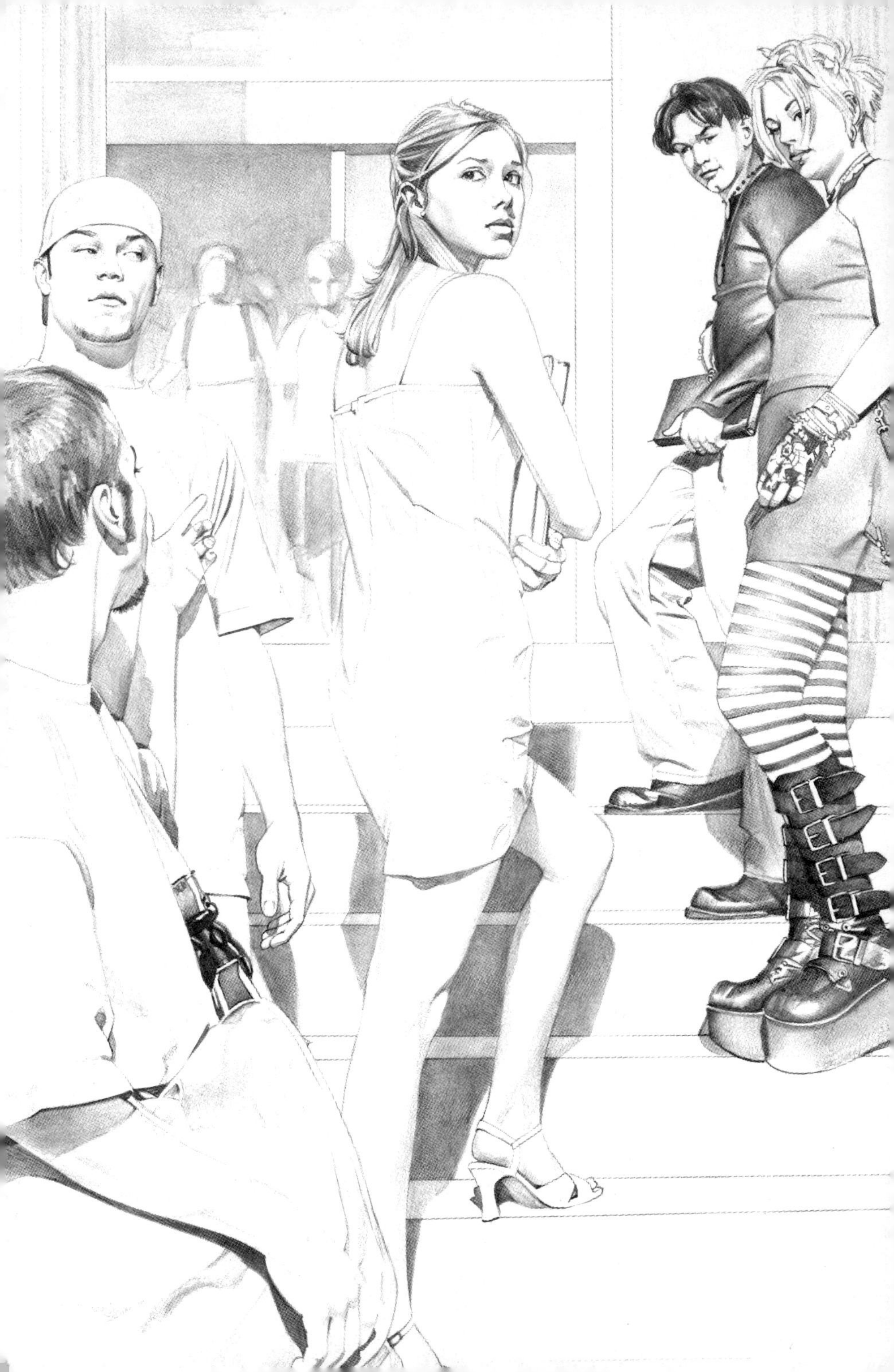

chapter 3

Wendy Gonzales was not waiting for Mary Jane on the corner as usual the next morning. So after about five minutes of standing alone in the cold wind, she just went off to school by herself.

That had happened a few times before, but in the past Mary Jane had known if her best friend wasn't feeling well the night before, or if she had a dentist appointment and wouldn't be in school until later. They'd usually spoken on the phone the night before, no matter how late Mary Jane's ballet class had been, or how long Wendy had been held hostage by the bratty Campbell kids whom she was always babysitting.

This time they didn't meet up until lunch.

"Hey, are you okay?" Mary Jane asked when she saw Wendy chatting away with Bernie Glick, who was to play Professor Henry Higgins to Wendy's Eliza Doolittle in My Fair Lady. Bernie was tall and thin, without much of a singing voice. He announced during the audition that his lack of traditional vocal abilities was perfectly acceptable, even preferred, since Rex Harrison, who originated the part in the movie, was no great shakes in the tune department either. And Rex had proved to be more than adequate in the role, thank you very much.

Mr. Toby had been unable to repress a grin at Bernie appointing himself Midtown High's resident Rex Harrison. He nodded, jotted down a few notes on his clipboard, and called out for the next person in line. But Bernie had a few things going for him. One, he did possess an uncanny air of self-importance that would be required for the role of Professor Higgins. The second, and perhaps most vital, thing Bernie had going for him was that only two other males had auditioned for the part, and neither of their voices had changed yet. It was one thing to have a non-singing Professor Higgins. Quite another to have the lines cracked in a squeaky soprano.

Bernie Glick had already established himself as something of a theatrical snob. Wendy and Mary Jane used to think he was absolutely hilarious. Once, when in English class, he answered the teacher's question in a pseudo-British accent, beginning his reply with, "Methinks Shakespeare had it right when he said 'A rose by any other name would smell as sweet'…" And he wasn't even trying to be funny.

That really cracked both of them up, and for the following week they began each conversation with "methinks."

The other advantage Bernie had was height. He was the only guy who auditioned who was taller than Wendy. They had giggled when the cast list was first posted and they saw that Bernie would be Wendy's leading man.

"You know what they say about backstage romances," Mary Jane had teased.

Wendy had been appalled by the thought. "As if!"

Now, however, it appeared Wendy was more than willing to take Bernie and his seemingly limitless collection of bow ties all too seriously.

Wendy turned to Mary Jane in the cafeteria, and for the briefest of moments MJ thought she saw a flash of irritation pass through her friend's pretty dark eyes. But then she smiled, her trademark dimples shining. "Hey, MJ!"

Bernie acknowledged Mary Jane with a barely perceivable bow, then with somber deliberation, he removed to his table to finish his taco.

"Guess what?" Wendy began excitedly.

"Did he ask you to the Winter Formal?"

Wendy frowned. "Who, Bernie?"

"No," she lowered her voice. "Dave Lipinski."

Again a fleeting look of annoyance, then, "Dave Lipinski? Oh, I'd forgotten all about him. No, the real news is that Bernie's going to grow a genuine beard in time for the production. Isn't that cool?"

"Methinks opening night will have to be postponed by a decade to get any decent growth on Sir Bernie's chin," Mary Jane said lightly in her own fake English accent.

The smile left Wendy's face. "He shaves, you know. He's been shaving since freshman year."

A weird, uncomfortable feeling went though Mary Jane, as if this person looked like Wendy, talked like Wendy, but was in fact a pod person sent from another planet. "Sorry," she mumbled.

"He's even shown me where he cut himself shaving." Wendy continued to defend Bernie's whiskers.

Mary Jane thought it best to change the subject. "Guess what? Peter asked me to the Winter Formal!"

Wendy shrugged, and at first she didn't say anything.

"Did you hear what I just said? Peter asked me to the dance," Mary Jane repeated, with slightly deflated excitement.

Wendy rolled her eyes. "Finally. I mean, really, it's not as if he was going to take anyone else. He's your boyfriend,

MJ. This is no big deal. I just can't believe he waited this long. Pretty rude, if you think about it."

Who WAS this person? And what had the aliens done with the real Wendy?

"I suppose that's one way to look at it," Mary Jane said with disappointment. She'd wanted Wendy to share her excitement, to grab her hand and start discussing what kind of dress she should wear.

Half the fun of getting invited to the Winter Formal was telling people. And if Wendy wasn't psyched, how could she herself be expected to get into the perfect prom zone?

Then she saw Peter walk into the lunchroom with a girl in thick glasses, impossibly mousy hair, and a fuzzy pink and purple striped sweater so ugly it had to be some kind of political statement. They were speaking intently, Peter nodding as the girl gestured with her hands. "Who's that with Peter?" Mary Jane asked.

Wendy glanced over her shoulder. "That? Oh, yeah, I sometimes forget you're still new here. That's Gwen Stacy, a total newspaper nerd. I hear she's really smart, but anyone wearing a sweater like that to a cutthroat place like high school could probably use a clue," she said.

"She sat out of gym for weeks because of poison ivy. I mean, really. She managed to get it, like, four times last spring. Talk about lame. Listen, I've got to go. Bernie and I need to discuss our characters a little more. See ya."

Then she was off.

"Oh, well," Mary Jane said to no one as she stood alone with her tray. For a moment she contemplated sitting down with Wendy and Bernie. It's not as if Wendy had actually banished her from their table, or held up a plastic fork and chanted "Mary Jane, be gone!" And she *was* in the musical.

Still, she felt like a total outsider with the theater crowd, all of whom seemed to embrace their carefully cultivated quirks as if they were performance art. There were about seven of them, the rotating standard cast for leads in all of the school productions. They were a strange lot, a few of them wearing tweed scarves throughout the day. MJ thought she overheard something about method acting. One kid always wore a puffy cap with the bill cocked to the side, like one of the Artful Dodger's sidekicks from *Oliver Twist*.

Nah. Mary Jane would have to find someplace else to sit. She looked around, weighing the advantages and disadvantages of each table before finally heading over to an empty one.

Odd. Since her very first day at Midtown she had eaten lunch with Wendy, either the two of them alone or with other people. No matter what, that had been a constant.

She settled at the table, opened her milk carton and glanced back at Peter. Gwen Stacy was staring at him as he spoke, her eyes wide behind the big, square glasses. Her mouth was set in a pursed smile, as if she was trying very hard not to grin broadly.

And then she reached up and began to twirl a strand of her lank hair, her focus never wavering from Peter's face.

Mary Jane put down the milk carton. With absolute certainty, beyond the slimmest shadows of the smallest doubts, she knew that Gwen Stacy had a major-league crush on Peter. It was so obvious, it was almost painful to see.

Just then Peter glanced casually at Mary Jane, and his own expression went from vague interest in whatever he was discussing with Gwen, to a total awareness of MJ. With a complete lack of self-consciousness, he simultaneously smiled, mouthed "Hi!" and waved at her with such energy, he looked like one of those guys who direct commercial airplanes on the runway.

It was slightly embarrassing; everyone knows you're not supposed to make any obvious gestures in the cafeteria. And she could have sworn she heard Wendy laughing just then.

Gwen followed Peter's line of vision leading to Mary Jane, suddenly releasing her hair from its flirtatious twirl. For a moment she just stared, as if frozen in time. Peter punched her shoulder, guy-to-guy, and began striding towards Mary Jane. It wasn't until then that Gwen's shoulders sagged, and all animation suddenly drained from her body. She stared across the lunchroom at her rival, then at Peter's back as he jauntily approached Mary Jane.

There was a sadness about her that was almost palpable, and Mary Jane felt a sharp stab of empathy.

Poor Gwen Stacy.

Peter was at her table. "Hi there," he said, sliding into the chair next to hers.

Gwen turned and fled the lunchroom.

"Gwen Stacy is madly in love with you," Mary Jane blurted.

"Huh?"

"I'm serious. Gwen Stacy really likes you."

"No way," he looked over his shoulder, but she was already gone. "She's my boss at the paper, Mary Jane. I mean, she's really smart and all, and a sweet kid. But she's one of those chicks who doesn't seem to notice the male population unless they can write a decent lead or snap a good picture."

"I wouldn't be so sure." MJ sipped the milk, then quickly put it back on the tray as she crinkled her nose. "Yuck. Is there some sort of law that requires cafeteria milk to be served at room temperature?"

Peter drummed his palm on the table. "Absolutely. The law was passed sometime after the Civil War to discourage mealtime enjoyment during school hours." He did a final ba-dum-dum on the table, glanced at the large wall clock, then stopped. "Hey, where's Wendy? She sick or something?"

"Nah. She's sitting over there with Bernie Glick discussing their characters for the musical." She tried to keep the hurt out of her voice.

Peter leaned back in his chair, raising an eyebrow. "What's there to discuss? He's the callous academic, and she's the spunky Cockney flower seller. They meet, they fight, they fall in love, they dance and sing."

"Yeah, well. I guess they're going for that extra bit of realism."

"A realistic musical. Just what the world is waiting for." He peered more closely at her. "You okay?"

"Sure." She looked over at Bernie and Wendy, who were laughing loudly in a theatrical, look-at-us way.

"Speaking of dance, would you like to go out to dinner before the Winter Formal? Maybe someplace special."

"Okay," she smiled as he stood up. "That would be nice. Especially if they serve cold milk."

"Great! Now I've gotta go. French test."

"Oh. Good luck, then."

"Yeah. Adios. Um, and I'll try to call you later."

Peter left, and Mary Jane contemplated her dismal lunch, from the soggy egg salad sandwich to the mottled banana. The best part may very well have been the tepid milk.

Wendy and Bernie laughed once again, but now they were joined by more theater kids. Mary Jane decided it didn't matter how gross her lunch was. She wasn't that hungry after all.

* * *

Despite her doubts, Mary Jane couldn't help but be excited by the first rehearsal for My Fair Lady.

At first she was slightly hesitant to go backstage, wondering if it would be too strange to see Wendy after the lunchroom brush-off, wondering of she would feel totally out of place.

Why had she even auditioned to begin with?

At least with ballet class she knew exactly what to do, and where she belonged. What was expected of her and how to make things work.

But it turned out she had nothing to worry about. Everyone else felt the same way, shrugging hellos, all a little embarrassed that they hadn't been given bigger parts, but delighted to have a role in any case.

Wendy and the other principles rehearsed their numbers and scenes in another room, just as the chorus members would be moving into the gym as soon as the stage crew started building the bigger sets.

She even knew a few of the kids in the chorus. Other than the ones who remained a little bitter about not being cast in a lead role ("I really think they should have allowed a female to play Henry Higgins," growled one girl, or "Why does Eliza have to sing if most of the guys don't?"), everyone was happy to be there.

The rehearsal started with the chorus director handing out music and playing a CD of the original production. After they finished following each song along with the musical score, the show's choreographer appeared.

"Ms. Krumplesteater?" Mary Jane said a little too loudly. "The volleyball coach?"

It didn't inspire confidence to see the choreographer in cargo shorts, a tee shirt that read "Floor Hockey Rocks!" and a big silver whistle around her thick neck. Which she wasn't afraid to use. She blew the whistle once, with gale force, a piercing screech.

"Okay, team," she began, clapping her hands, speaking from the side of her mouth so the whistle could remain in place. "Let's get up here and start moving!"

She motioned to the stage, and after exchanging perplexed glances, the chorus scrambled to their places.

"One and two and..."

With that she switched the music back on and began a peculiar march-like walk, more of an orchestrated lurch, to the strains of "Get Me to the Church on Time."

Mr. Toby watched for a few moments, and with obvious pain, quickly left the stage.

On every alternate step, Ms. Krumplesteater, who was also the driver's ed instructor, blew the whistle lightly.

"Keep it up, folks! And one and a two and a...." They walked in dutiful, if disorganized, circles.

"Excellent! That is just what I'm looking for!"

"What's that — an utter mess?" Mary Jane said to the person next to her. Unfortunately, her voice carried.

"Excuse me?" Ms. Krumplesteater, hands clasped behind her back, marched over to her. "Did you just say something, Miss...?"

"Watson. And no, not really."

"Would you please share it with the rest of us?" She flicked off the CD player.

Mary Jane felt her face redden. "I just said, um, 'What's that — an *arabesque*?'"

Ms. Krumplesteater straightened and let the whistle flop from her mouth. "An *arabesque*? That has something to do with ballet." Her eyes narrowed. "So do you know anything about dance?"

Mary Jane nodded. "Yeah, a little."

"Interesting. Maybe you can be my assistant if I happen to need any help."

"Sure. I'd be more than happy to..."

But before she could finish the whistle was back in Ms. Krumplesteater's mouth, blowing a staccato command. "Okay, team! Let's make a big circle!"

And with that they walked in time to the rest of the show's music, the whistle keeping its own bizarro beat.

The Manhattan School of Ballet was looking better by the minute.

* * *

It was almost ten-thirty at night, when Mary Jane came to the conclusion that there was nothing more insidious than hanging out at home and waiting for the telephone to ring.

So she attempted to keep herself busy after her homework was finished by logging online to get a jumpstart on the history paper due in a few weeks.

"Let's see," she mumbled to herself, scrolling ahead. "Civil War, Gettysburg." She clicked and waited for the topic to appear. Instead an instant message sign popped up in the corner.

HotCop54 wants to send you an Instant Message. Will you accept?

She frowned, "HotCop54?" But she clicked on "yes" anyway, wondering if it could be someone from school.

Hey, baby! How R ya?

"Who is this?" She typed.

It's me, dollface. I miss you.

It definitely wasn't Peter. He wasn't the "dollface" type.

How's about an old-fashioned kiss?

"Yuck," she said to the screen. Then she typed in, "How's about an old-fashioned slap?"

Love it when u get frisky! :-) Be sure to catch u later!

HotCop54 vanished, and when she tried to ask again who it was, the computer said that he was no longer online.

Curious, she checked the Member Directory to see if there was a listing, but apparently HotCop54 was a little less bold than his messages would indicate. In fact, there was nothing on him, no hobbies, age, location or even gender.

Weird.

Now it was close to eleven. It was late, especially for a school night, but she couldn't resist.

Biting her lip, she punched in the numbers. A woman answered.

"Hello."

"Oh, hi, Mrs. Gonzales. This is Mary Jane. Is Wendy home?"

"Hello, Mary Jane! How have you been?"

"I'm fine."

"Wendy isn't here. Actually, she should have been back about an hour ago, but she's over at Bernie Glick's house with some other kids working on their parts. And congratulations on making the play yourself! Good job, Mary Jane! Wendy said you really did well in the audition."

"Thank you, Mrs. Gonzales. But I didn't do nearly as well as Wendy did. She was amazing!"

"Well, she sure practiced in the shower long enough, that's for sure. She must have been the cleanest kid at the auditions. Anyway, I'll tell her you called. Bye now."

"Bye, and thank you."

She hung up the phone, feeling a little off. It just didn't seem right, as if they were in a fight, but they weren't. The only thing different was that Wendy was the lead in the musical, and Mary Jane wasn't.

Maybe she had been the cause of the rift? Was it possible she hadn't been as good of a friend as she should have been? She had congratulated Wendy, of course, and was genuinely pleased when her friend got the part.

Or was she?

Just then the phone rang, and she picked up before the first ring had stopped echoing.

"Wendy?" She asked excitedly.

"Sorry, it's only Pete," he laughed on the other end. There were car horns in the background.

"Hey, Tiger," she smiled. "Where are you?"

"In the city, just around the corner from the subway on East Fifty-Third Street. I just wanted to know how your practice went. Or rehearsal. Or whatever they call it in the world of thee-ah-ter," he said, doing his best Bernie Glick impersonation. "I wanted to call you before it was too late, and...whoops. I just looked at my watch. It already *is* too late. Sorry!"

"No, that's okay. I was still awake. Glad you called, though."

"Me too. So how was it?"

"I'm not sure. Fine, I guess. Just different from what I expected." She wondered if she should mention her doubts about the whole thing, but decided against it. Peter calling from a payphone was not the time to engage in a long conversation.

"It will get better, I'm sure. And I'll bet you were the best dancer, right?"

"Not sure if you'd call that dancing," she admitted. "Hey, what are you doing out so late? This is a school night, Mister. Your Aunt May must be frantic."

"Nah, she's okay. I was just trying to find a decent story, maybe one for the school paper. Or better yet, for the *Daily Bugle.*"

"Oh, Peter, really," she sighed. "What kind of story were you looking for?"

"Well, um. This sounds crazy, but I heard someone say the Spider-Man was prowling in Manhattan, and I thought I might catch a glimpse of the guy. Maybe even get a picture and an interview."

"Peter, really. If professional reporters are having trouble getting this person, he doesn't want to be seen. Be careful. You've seen the headlines, nobody knows anything about this guy. He could be some sort of criminal himself, a thief or murderer or something."

Peter began laughing.

"I'm serious! What if he's a terrorist? A sick-o terror-ist in tights."

"What about the tights?" He had stopped laughing.

"Nothing. You've got to admit it's pretty weird, this guy climbs walls dressed in ballet tights."

"They're not ballet tights. They're, like, ski tights. Thicker than ballet tights."

"Ski tights?" Now she started giggling.

"Yeah. Like what the Olympic guys wear when they compete. They are very masculine ski, eh, leggings."

"Peter, 'masculine' and 'leggings' do not belong in the same sentence."

"Whatever," he snapped.

"What's wrong?"

"Nothing."

"Come on, tell me."

"It's just that. Well. Cripes, MJ, nobody is giving this guy a chance! I mean, all he's done is stop a bunch of crimes..."

"He *claims* to stop the crimes," she interrupted. "Some people think he may be involved, as a distraction to the police."

"Who thinks that?"

"I don't know. This guy I heard on the radio this morning."

"What guy?"

"You know, Lenny Holiday on Z-Tone. That morning show he does."

"He thinks Spider-Man is a criminal?"

"I can't remember if that's what he said, or if it's what a caller said. Does it really –" She was interrupted by a police siren wailing through the phone.

"No, I guess not. Listen, MJ, gotta go! See ya tomorrow!" Click, then the dial tone.

Mary Jane scratched her head. "Weird," she said to no one. And with that she went to sleep.

* * *

Mary Jane turned up the radio as she brushed her teeth the next morning.

"Ladies and gentleman, we have a surprise guest with us here in the studio," chuckled Lenny Holiday, the shock jock on Z-Tone. He made the usual silly noises, the grunts and rattles and whizzing. "And I'll give you a hint: He's wearing red and blue tights!"

"They are not tights, Lenny." His voice was muffled, as if behind a mask. "They're ski leggings."

"Well, they're something else, Spidey. Mind if I call you Spidey?"

"Sure, Lenny. Go ahead."

"Now they have an interesting design, these...what did you call them?"

"Leggings. For male skiers."

"Right. Leggings. Anyway, they seem to have a sort of spider web design. So I have a question, a chicken-or-the-egg kind of question. So what came first, the cool leggings with the spider design, or your name Spider-Man?"

Mary Jane couldn't believe her ears! She spit out the toothpaste and called Peter's house right away.

"Hello," said Aunt May, a smile in her voice.

"Hi! Mrs. Parker, may I please speak to Peter? This is Mary Jane."

"Good morning, dear. I'm afraid Peter went to school early this morning. He said he had a bunch of film to develop in the newspaper darkroom."

"Really? I didn't know the darkroom would be open that early."

"Apparently so, my dear."

"Well, I'll catch up with him later then. Oh, and sorry for calling so early."

"Not at all. Good-bye, Mary Jane."

"Bye," she hung up.

But she couldn't wait to get to school to let Peter know his hero Spider-Man had been on the radio!

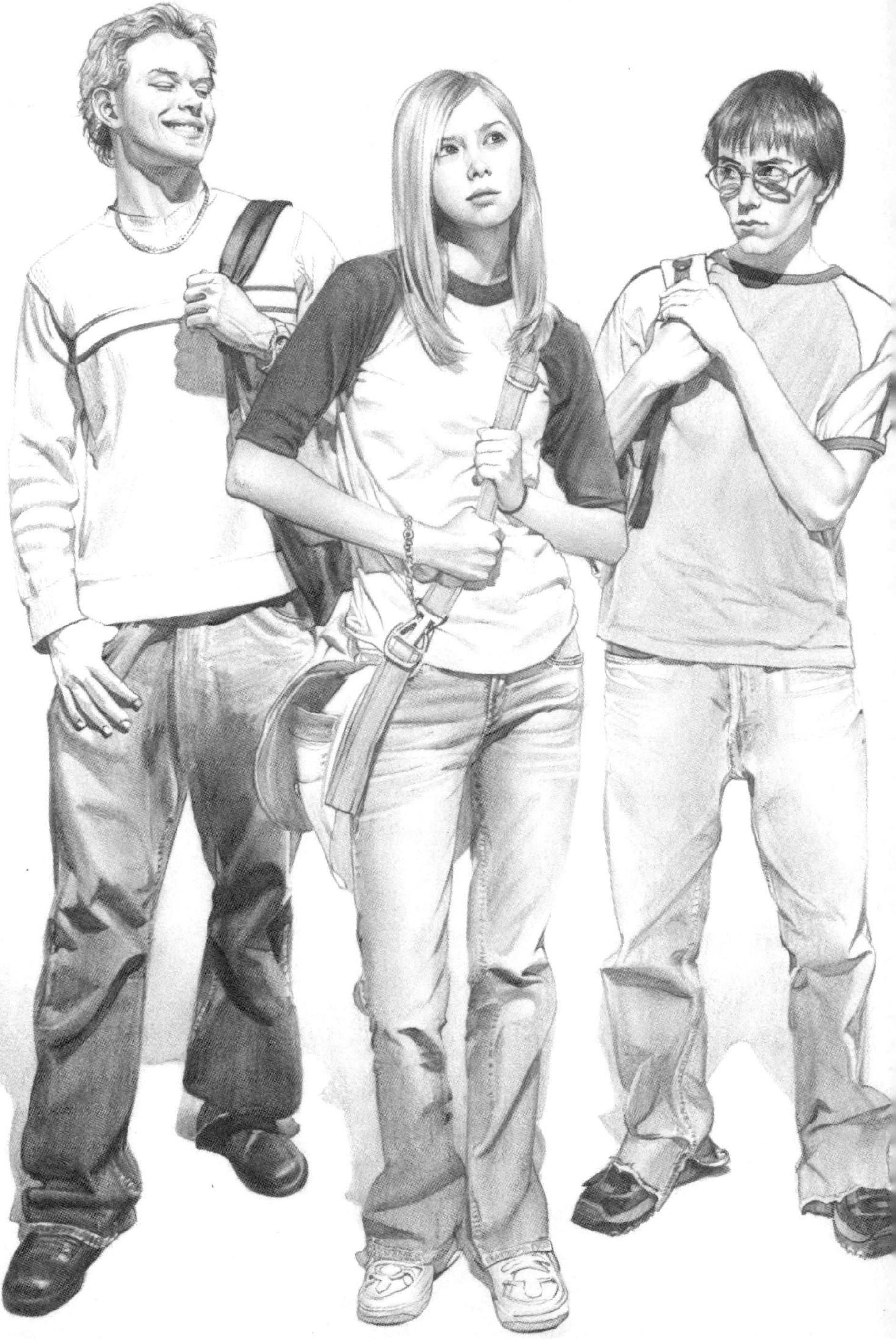

chapter 4

It soon became was one of those days that was best forgotten.

And funnily enough, that's exactly how she started the school day: forgetting. First about the Physics test, which she had somehow managed to erase from her memory on Monday. Everyone else was prepared, down to their sharpened No. 2 pencils and their formula sheets, all neatly readied the night before. Mary Jane had a pink metallic gel pen with a pom-pom dangling on the end (a joke gift from Wendy) and, of course, a dazed expression on her face.

To put it mildly, the test did not go well.

It was a difficult exam to begin with. Even Marvin Ling moaned several times and broke a pencil lead in his frustration. Exiting the classroom, she did her best to ignore all the right answers she had so spectacularly managed to miss.

"What did you get for question five?"

Uh, how about a smiley face and the doodle of a dog wearing a top hat?

"Anyone know question eight on the back?"

Yes. That would be a flower pot with daisies, thank you very much. Also a cross-eyed man with glasses and a funny nose. And don't forget the series of three-dimensional boxes in the corner.

Extra credit.

And that was not even the worst part of the day. Right after the physics test she ran into Peter.

"Hey! I tried to call you this morning..."

"Sorry, I've got to run. I was late this morning, didn't get to school until second period," he said as he walked backwards towards his next class.

"But I thought..."

"Hey, I just heard Duffy is giving a pop quiz in English."

"You're kidding!"

"Nope. *The Age of Innocence*. Edith Wharton," he shouted just as he turned the corner.

"No way!" She had intended to read the assigned chapters. Really she had.

But at least English was sixth period, right after lunch. If she skimmed the chapters then maybe she could...

"Hey, Mary Jane!" Harry Osborn grabbed her arm. "About Saturday. I was thinking we could all..."

"Hi, Harry," she muttered. She'd seen the movie version of the book a few years earlier. Maybe that would help. Unless of course it was totally different from the book.

Harry continued walking by her side. "Did you tell Peter about Saturday? He wasn't in homeroom this morning."

The bell blasted.

"I've got to go," she said, clutching her books and running for History.

"Okay! See you later."

Mary Jane was always amazed by how loud the bell was when it bounced off the glazed bricks and metal lockers of the hallway, and her ears were still ringing when she got to her next class.

She was only a little late for History. Which meant she only missed the beginning part. The part where the teacher explained the question on the pop quiz she sprung on the class. The essay question. As in, no multiple choice.

"Aw, no..." Mary Jane moaned.

"It's on Gettysburg," Amy what's-her-name said under her breath. "You know, the address place."

Great. This was the one quiz of the day she could have aced, if only she hadn't been sidetracked the night before by that creepy HotCop54.

If she ever found out who HotCop54 was, she would sincerely love to send him to a new address himself. A very hot place, with flames licking at his feet. Preferably with pitchforks piercing his flesh.

She pulled out her trusty pink pen and began to write, the pom-pom swinging as she jotted down everything she could recall seeing on the Web site about Gettysburg.

Then something amazing happened.

She actually remembered a bunch of random facts! She'd scanned the Web site more closely than she had thought. Lincoln gave the famous address at the dedication to the graveyard there. And the battle had taken place over several hot days, including July 4th. In 1863. The Union won and someone — was it Robert E. Lee? Someone important ate some bad peaches and got sick. And....

That's right when the pen ran out of ink.

Of course she didn't have a spare.

And of course if she hadn't covered her physics test with a bunch of meaningless metallic pink doodles, she would have had plenty of ink to fake her way through meaningless facts on Gettysburg.

"Amy, do you have an extra pen?" Mary Jane whispered just as another bunch of thoughts came into her head. The

Battle of Little Round Top! Pickett's Last Charge! She was a veritable quiz show cheat sheet on Gettysburg facts!

"Shhhhh!" Amy hissed.

"Miss Watson, do you have a question?" The teacher asked.

"Um, I need to borrow a pen or pencil. My ink ran out." She waved the pom-pom in the air.

"This is a good lesson for you, Miss Watson. You must always come prepared."

"But—"

The teacher snatched away her paper.

Mary Jane watched helplessly as everyone else, their tongues jutting from their mouths, wrote away.

At least next period was lunch, she sighed.

* * *

The only thing worse than having lunch be the only highlight of your pathetic day is having lunch be the highlight of your pathetic day, *and* forgetting to bring lunch money to school in the first place.

Oh, well. She wasn't hungry anyway, certainly not in the mood to chow down after a disastrous morning like that. And the warring scents of the lunchroom — old salami meets tuna salad meets peanut butter meets vegetable soup — made her more than happy to skip the Midtown High dining experience.

So she settled herself in a remote corner of the cafeteria and pulled out her copy of *The Age of Innocence*. She began reading, trying to get into the characters and the story, but finding it hard not to listen to the shouts of kids on the other side of the room, or the conversation about the swimming team behind her. About the girl who just found a long black hair imbedded deep within her mystery meatloaf.

Turning the page, she glanced up to see Gwen Stacy walking between tables. She was staring straight ahead in the time-honored method of avoiding being noticed. Her complete solitude all but screamed out.

Today the poor thing was wearing a bulky orange and brown sweater with a pink turtleneck underneath. Was her entire family colorblind, or just fashion-challenged? And she was wearing those same square glasses. They looked as if they belonged to an elderly man with a very large face and very bad eyes. As for her hair, well. Between the monster glasses and the color barf sweater, it didn't seem to matter that her hair was the shade of cafeteria-brown gravy, and that it had all the body and style of last Wednesday's spaghetti special.

Poor Gwen Stacy.

She was about to return to her book when she saw something terrible. A mere three or four steps from Gwen Stacy's intended path was an old, slimy banana peel.

Mary Jane's mouth opened in a stunned "O" of horror. Gwen's chin was raised, her eyes straight forward, avoiding contact with anyone else. Eager to get to a seat, any seat, without drawing undue attention to herself.

One foot, the next foot. One more step and...

"Gwen! Watch out!" Mary Jane shouted.

Everything happened in slow motion, like distorted surveillance camera footage of a crime scene.

Gwen's head spun in the direction of Mary Jane's cry, just as her bright orange tray flew into the air. It was really amazing the velocity of the thing, of how the macaroni and cheese — always lumped together on the plate as one solid mass — was able to launch into the atmosphere and separate, just in time to cover most of Gwen's hair and sweater.

The carton of chocolate milk, the very same container that is impossible to open when you're ready to drink, was even more impressive. It burst open with the joyful spray of a holiday fountain, covering those massive glasses of hers with a thick layer of foam and chocolate, then dripping off the end of her nose.

The orange tray hit her once on the shoulder as it bounced to the floor.

And finally there was the lime Jell-O, the little bowl of quivering emerald cubes. Mary Jane's first thought, detached with complete shock as the nightmare scene unfolded, was "Who on earth eats the lime Jell-O?" That was but a momentary thought. Her second thought was, "Wow — they really put a lot of whipped cream on the Jell-O."

Defying the known laws of physics, a sore topic to MJ that particular day, the green Jell-O demonstrated a unique ability to take flight on its own. As if piloted by some twisted, perverse gremlin, the gelatin remained airborne the longest. The Kitty Hawk of desserts seemed to circle once before landing directly on top of Gwen's head. Complete with whipped cream and the obligatory maraschino cherry.

Ironically enough, her foot had completely sidestepped the banana peel. Had Mary Jane remained silent, this disaster never would have occurred.

There was a terrible hush in the cafeteria. It became so still she could hear the low hum of the big fluorescent lights overhead. The distant ping of the cash register at the end of the food line.

And then came the inevitable. The laughter.

But it wasn't just laughter. It was something more, something much deeper. It was the sound of kids laughing with relief because their greatest secret fear had finally happened, only not to them. It was the giddy, out-of-proportion howl that for the moment, they were all off the hook. They had all been spared this humiliation.

Then it became the full-throttle laughter because this had happened to Gwen Stacy. And if there was anyone at Midtown it was okay to laugh at openly and brazenly, it was Gwen Stacy.

Gwen stood motionless for a moment, as if paralyzed by the enormity of what had just happened.

Mary Jane didn't think twice. She swept up her book, backpack and purse and ran to Gwen's side.

"Are you okay?" She asked stupidly, shouting to be heard over the sounds of the general hilarity.

Gwen did not answer. She simply stood motionless, her eyes filling with tears behind those square, chocolate-covered lenses.

Mary Jane hooked her arm through Gwen's and started to pull her out of the lunchroom.

"Hey, she's got to clean this mess up!" It was some dweeby freshman lunch monitor. Mary Jane glared as they passed. "Nevermind," he smiled nervously. "I'll get it. No problem."

Once in the hallway they passed people who were just entering the lunchroom, people who hadn't witnessed the calamity. They stared in openmouthed wonder at the sight of Mary Jane scurrying towards the nearest girls' room with a nearly catatonic Gwen slathered in the lunch special.

"We'll get you all cleaned up. You'll see," Mary Jane reassured, although she didn't really believe it herself.

They pushed through the doors of the girls' room, and luckily, it was empty.

"Oh, no," Gwen finally croaked.

"It's fine. You'll be fine." Even MJ realized she was using the same tone doctors use on terminal patients in TV shows.

Gwen blinked. "You're Mary Jane, aren't you?"

"Yeah, I am."

"Peter Parker's girlfriend, right?"

"Yep. And I'm so sorry. I thought you were about to step on a banana peel, that's why I shouted."

"That was *you*?" Her voice was hollow, disbelieving.

"I'm afraid so. Here, let's get this sweater off you first."

They pulled it over her head, and Mary Jane took it to the sink.

"Is it ruined?" Gwen asked.

Mary Jane resisted the urge to reply, "Hard to tell." Instead she smiled with false optimism. "With a little soap and water, it will be as good as new."

"Good. My dad would kill me."

Gwen went to another sink. "Oh, no," she breathed when she saw herself.

"Hey, listen. It's not as bad as it looks. Rinse off your face and we can reapply your makeup."

Gwen removed her glasses. As if she had been wearing goggles, there were two perfect squares of clean skin over her eyes. "My glasses are really messed up."

"Yeah, I know."

She placed them carefully on the shelf over the sink, then washed her face and splashed her hair with water, picking out the major chunks.

"I hear Cheese Wiz is great for the hair," Mary Jane said conversationally. "I mean it really makes it shiny and all."

Gwen turned to her slowly, frown lines creasing her forehead. Mary Jane looked up and their eyes met.

Then Gwen Stacy smiled. "Sure. I just read about the mac-and-cheese hair treatment last week." She shook her head and a few pieces of pasta fell to the ground.

They both just stared at the floor. And suddenly, Gwen giggled. Not a hearty laugh, just a weak, survivor's giggle. "I guess it could have been worse. I could have gone to school in my underwear."

"Or without it," Mary Jane said with meaning.

Then they both did start laughing, self-consciously at first, then with genuine humor.

"You're lucky you didn't eat it," Mary Jane said while wiping off Gwen's purse. "I hear there was a hair in the meatloaf."

"Now *that* would have been nasty." Gwen rubbed a soapy paper towel over her hair. "Oh, man. What am I going to do?"

Mary Jane looked up, about to answer, when she stopped.

Gwen turned to her, her arms held at her side. Without the hideous sweater, with just the tight pink turtleneck, Gwen Stacy had a knockout figure! The shirt was tucked into very okay jeans, hip-hugging and revealing her more-than-okay form.

Mary Jane was about to say something, when she looked up at Gwen's face.

Was it possible? Behind those big, square, man-glasses was...a really pretty face!

"Gwen Stacy, do you have any idea how cute you are?"

Gwen blushed furiously, more embarrassed now than she had been in the lunchroom. "Please don't make fun of me."

"But I'm not! Really! Wait, do you mind if I do something?"

"What else are you going to do to me?"

"Not to you, for you," Mary Jane said warmly. With that she opened her own backpack and pulled out a little zippered makeup case. "My mother, you see, is a Skye Bleu salesgal."

"No kidding? My mother used to wear Skye Bleu cosmetics all the time."

"Ah, you say that in the past tense," Mary Jane said lightly, peering into the kit to find precisely what she needed. "Don't tell me your mother abandoned the world of Skye Bleu for the greener pastures of another brand."

"Nope. She abandoned me and my dad for greener pastures. Period."

Mary Jane stopped, the mascara wand poised in midair. "I know what you mean. My dad did the same thing, years ago. It sucks."

"Sure does."

"Hey, do you need to wear those glasses all the time?"

Gwen shrugged. "Not really, I'm just used to them. They're comfortable, in a way."

"Well, comfortable or not, they're pretty gross at the moment. Maybe you can try to do without them for a bit."

"Okay."

There were still deep indentations on her nose marking where the glasses had been.

Then Mary Jane smiled. "After I do your face, mind if I fiddle with your hair a bit?"

"Go ahead, fiddle away. I just hope for your sake you're not lactose intolerant. There's a whole lot of cheese and milk up there."

"Don't forget the whipped cream."

"How could I forget?" Gwen nodded, then closed her eyes and let Mary Jane go to work.

* * *

Fifteen minutes later, Mary Jane stepped back from her handiwork.

And she was absolutely stunned. More so than she had been at the lunchroom spill itself.

Gwen was afraid to look in the mirror. "Is it that bad?"

Wordlessly, Mary Jane took her by the shoulders and spun her towards the mirror.

Gwen gasped.

She wasn't simply cute, or passable. Gwen Stacy was nothing short of total babedom.

"My dad will kill me!" But as she spoke she touched her face, as if reassuring herself that the image reflected back in the mirror was indeed her own.

Mary Jane folded her arms in satisfaction. Really, though, it hadn't taken much to turn Gwen into Midtown's own Cinderella.

Aside from her figure, which most girls would inflict personal torture to achieve, Gwen's face was beyond pretty. Her features, small and even, were quite lovely once the glasses were gone. Her eyes were an incredible shade of deep blue, almost sapphire, and her lashes were thick and plentiful. They were just light, so without a bit of mascara they were all but invisible.

Mary Jane used a few tricks her mother had taught her, such as applying darker eyeshadow in the hollow of the socket, making the eyes appear much larger. And brushing a bit of blush on the forehead and chin as well as on the apples of the cheeks. Then she used a little lip liner on the edges to make her lips look a bit fuller, filling in the rest with a very natural-looking mauve gloss.

After that there was her hair, which, in spite of having most of the major food groups represented, was actually thick and soft. The major problem was the style, just hanging there, but it was certainly nothing that a halfway decent cut wouldn't fix. For the time being, Mary Jane merely pulled her hair back and up into a soft twist, fastened with a pretty clip she had in her backpack.

"Wow," was all Gwen could say.

"That about sums it up," Mary Jane agreed.

The bell rang. And suddenly it was Mary Jane's turn to go pale.

"What's wrong?" Gwen asked with a smile, staring at herself as she spoke, tilting her head at different angles.

"I have a pop quiz. And I've already had a rough day."

"*You've* had a rough day?" Gwen raised her gently arched eyebrows.

"Yeah, well." Mary Jane leaned over to gather her things. "Um, you might want to skip the sweater. It will take a while to dry, and I'd hate to see you catch cold."

"That, and the fact that it's a completely hideous waste of perfectly good lambswool. Just think, someplace a lamb is bald. For this."

Mary Jane straightened, not sure if she heard right, as Gwen rolled up the sweater and stuffed it into her backpack.

"I know how ugly they are. But you see, my dad buys them, and he's already so sensitive about it just being the two of us, you know? Anyway, he figures if it's bright and colorful, it must be for a girl."

"Well, it's bright and colorful all right," Mary Jane said as the last of the sweater disappeared.

"What's the quiz on?"

"Huh?"

"The pop quiz. What's it on?"

"Oh, you mean the one I'm about to fail? It's on *The Age of Innocence* by Edith Wharton."

Gwen grinned. "Only one of my favorite books."

"First five chapters?"

"No problem."

"And do you have a pen or pencil I can borrow?"

Gwen reached into her backpack and produced a small, zippered pencil pouch similar to Mary Jane's Skye Bleu makeup case. "I know, I know. Total nerd patrol." She handed MJ two pens, one blue and one black, and two perfectly sharpened pencils.

"Thanks," Mary Jane said.

"You're welcome. So, *The Age of Innocence*. One thing you need to keep in mind is that Wharton herself was part of that world in the eighteen seventies, upper-crust New York and Newport and all that. Names were more important than money."

Mary Jane smiled wryly, thinking of her old private-school days. "Sounds familiar."

"Yeah, so you have Newland Archer, semi-rich guy from old family, engaged to May Welland, same thing. But Newland falls for May's cousin, the exotically beautiful Countess Olenska..."

The two girls emerged from the ladies' room, deep in discussion. Neither took any notice of the stares, gawks, and almost comical double takes that followed them down the hallway.

* * *

By the end of the day, the big gossip at Midtown High was not the brawl between the captain of the football team and some guy who had been passing notes to his girlfriend. It wasn't the news that the biology teacher, Mr. Moinester, was retiring the following year. It wasn't even the tale of the lunchtime pratfall.

Instead, the major gossip was about the new hot chick with Mary Jane Watson. The boys' locker room was especially buzzing.

"Wait a sec, I thought the new hot chick was Mary Jane Watson."

"Well, sure. But there's this other new girl, a total hottie. Wearing a bright pink turtleneck."

"Dude, I love turtlenecks on chicks!"

And also in the girls' locker room.

"Oh my gosh, did you see Gwen Stacy this afternoon?"

"Sure, with Mary Jane. I've always liked Gwen. Haven't you?"

"Of course, what's not to like? Maybe we should invite her to the mall with us on Saturday."

Mary Jane couldn't help but feel somewhat pleased with herself for the transformation, although in truth she owed a lot to Gwen. Thanks to her crash course on Edith Wharton, there was a good chance she did pretty well on the English quiz.

At rehearsal that afternoon, she motioned to Wendy. She couldn't wait to recount Gwen's makeover.

But once again the leads were practicing in another room. Wendy shrugged and held up her fingers as a handset. "I'll call you tonight," she mouthed.

Mary Jane nodded. Maybe it had all been her imagination, the Wendy thing. With a deep sigh she joined the others in the chorus, walking in an endless circle on the command of a whistle-blowing volleyball coach.

Like the rest of the kids wrapped up in their reenactment of another world, a simpler time, she had no idea that just outside the Midtown campus, the Spider-Man was about to risk his life to stop another crime.

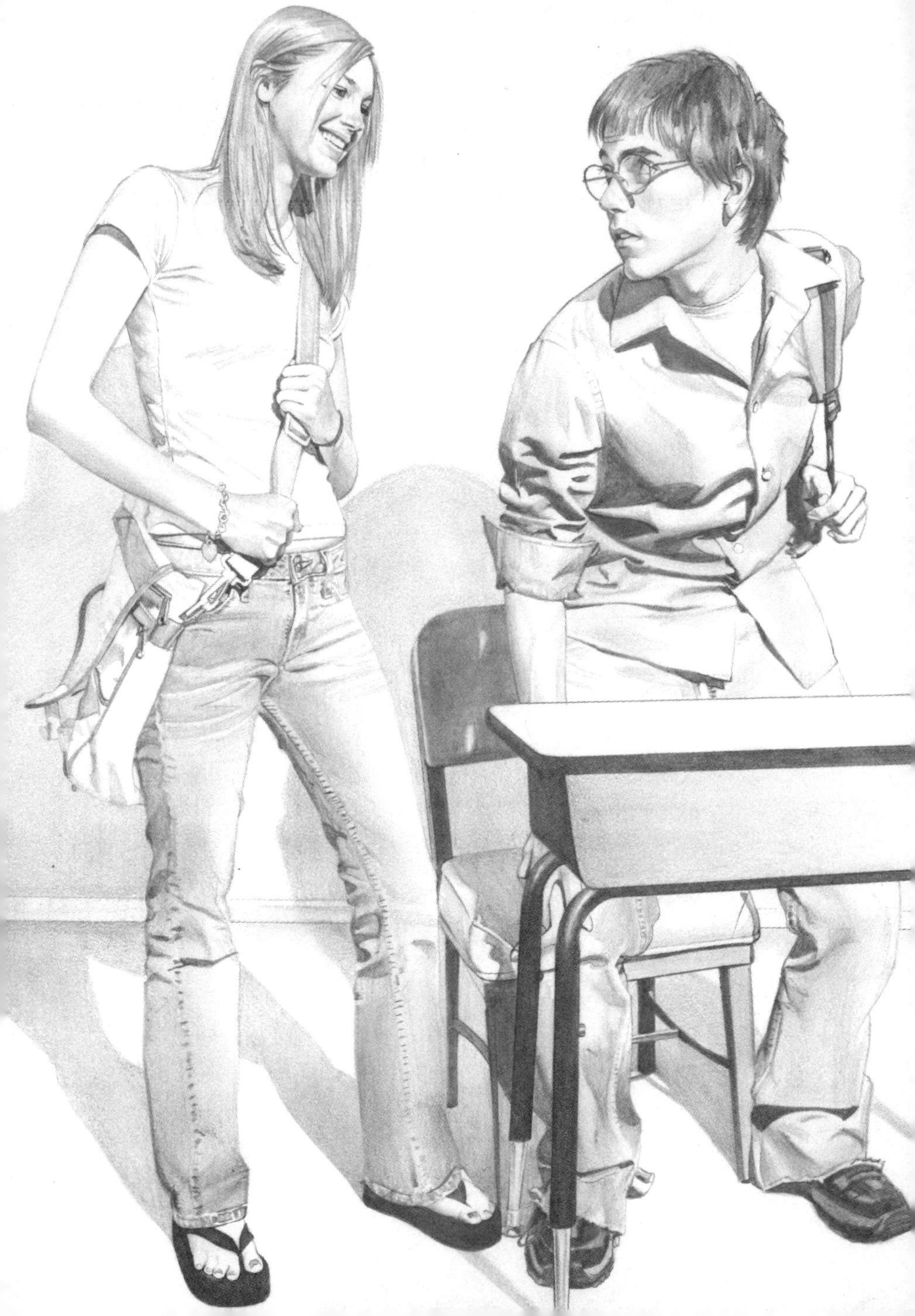

chapter 5

Mary Jane Watson had always promised herself she'd never judge people solely on their looks. She had known enough wealthy, beautiful people in her early childhood to learn that what was reflected on people's outside didn't always match what was within. She prided herself on her belief that it was a person's inner qualities that made all the difference. Physical appearance should be secondary to personal integrity, to intelligence and humor, to wisdom and kindness. And yet, as she stared at the front page of the *Daily Bugle*, she couldn't help but wonder...was it terribly wrong for her to notice how fantastic Spider-Man looked in his tights? Or ski leggings?

After all, the guy had apparently stopped some thug from carjacking an SUV from a single mother with her kid at a Queens gas station. That was something to be applauded at the very least, perhaps an insight to the man's character. Here was a person who not only disapproved of the victimization of the innocent, but also placed himself in physical peril to thwart such abuse. Not only was he willing to allow himself to face genuine danger, he was also unafraid to risk the jeers and taunts of the general public. And to many, he was an object of scorn, including politicians and law enforcement officials. They were perplexed by this mysterious person who had come so suddenly and so fearlessly on the scene.

People doubted his motives, wondered who he really was, what his genuine purpose could possibly be. Nobody could fathom that perhaps he actually wanted to help people, to spring into action when others were content to offer nothing but lip service.

But from everything Mary Jane could see, that was just it. Nothing prompted him other than an overwhelming desire to make things right, to aid the helpless. She herself had encountered him once before, when she had rushed into traffic distracted and upset. Thanks to Spider-Man, she emerged from the incident in one piece. And with a desire to meet him again.

But clearly there was more to this person than just a great body and cling wrap attire. And when she'd heard him speaking on the radio, he'd seemed such a normal guy. Funny, even, with a modest demeanor.

How weird was it that both Peter and Spider-Man had been so adamant about calling the tights "leggings?" Such a male thing, she supposed, like when little boys call their toys "action figures" instead of dolls, or leather man-purses "totes."

It was amusing, actually, that a few months earlier, she'd been convinced that Peter *was* Spider-Man.

As if!

All she had was some compelling (to her, anyway) circumstantial evidence. Such as the fact that he had borrowed her red and blue dance tights (not leggings, but indisputable, jazz hands-inducing tights) just before Spider-Man's first appearance. He returned them days later all stretched out of shape. At the time he claimed it was because his Aunt May had done something peculiar with the laundry.

Like what — getting an eight hundred pound gorilla to wear them until they'd never spring back to their original shape?

Or that whenever Spider-Man appeared, Peter seemed to vanish, if only to return a few moments later. It was almost like clockwork. Spider-Man there, Peter gone. And as much as she had seen of both guys, she could never recall seeing him and having Peter at her side simultaneously.

Yeah, *that* was rock-solid proof.

Which only proved was that she was not the only chick at Midtown High who was completely delusional about guys. After all, even her best friend Wendy was convinced her new costar Bernie Glick was the greatest thing since chips and dip.

Still, there was something more to Peter. Something deeper and elusive, secrets he was reluctant to reveal. Sometimes she would catch glimpses of deep sadness that would cross his features at odd times, then disappear just as quickly. Sometimes it was a darkness that would suddenly flicker in his eyes, so ephemeral that she would often think it was her own imagination. Yet she knew it wasn't.

But that only made sense. What kid whose parents were killed in a plane crash, and whose uncle had just been murdered on his own front steps wouldn't have a few issues to resolve?

So Mary Jane pushed those thoughts from her mind and determined instead to concentrate on the more important issue at hand. Namely, how very great Spider-Man looked in tights.

* * *

As the night of the Winter Formal rapidly approached, Mary Jane found she could think of nothing else.

Her mom had found a dress pattern similar to the amazing one featured in a recent fashion magazine. It was beautifully simple, with a plain bodice held up with by slenderest wisps of straps, nipped at the waist, then gathered gently in the back into a cluster of folds that had a slight bustle effect without looking like an all-out lump. In the magazine it was pictured in black silk, to show off the honking diamond necklace the model was wearing. Madeline Watson, however, was of the firm (and old-fashioned, Mary Jane thought) belief that girls under twenty-one should never wear black unless to a funeral, and no one should ever wear a honking diamond necklace before eight in the evening. Period.

"Okay," Mary Jane had sighed after her initial excitement at seeing the pattern had ebbed. "I'll stash the jewels back in the vault until after dessert."

At that her mom had merely smiled, and pulled out the most gorgeous, deep green satin material Mary Jane had ever seen! It was even more stunning than the fabric in the magazine, and she could imagine how the lights would reflect off the dress, how it would work so well with her auburn hair.

Just as she was about to ooh and ahh about how she already had the perfect shoes, her mother went into her bedroom and emerged with a long, red velvet box. "I said no diamonds before evening. There is no such rule about pearls."

Mary Jane gasped as her mother clicked the box open. Her mother's pearls! The special gift her dad had given her the day they were married!

How many times had her mother held on to them no matter how badly they needed ready cash? Mary Jane used to imagine it was because of the way her mother must still feel about her father. A lost love that had left her with one solitary, tangible vestige of how she had once been adored.

Instead it was for the very practical reason that if they were ever really in a pinch, they could always sell — or, as her mother said, hock — the necklace in a moment's notice.

"Oh, Mom. I can't," she said, touching each iridescent orb with reverence, savoring the silken feel.

"Please. I had them restrung for you."

Mary Jane looked up at her mother and swallowed. "Really?"

"Yes," her mom looked away and then looked back at her daughter unflinchingly. "Please wear these. It will cleanse away the bad memories. And then maybe sometime I can wear them again."

Mary Jane nodded. "Thank you," she whispered.

"Guess we'd better get started on the dress. I mean, it does have to stand up to the pearls." Her mother stood up.

"Mom, thank you again," Mary Jane kissed her on the cheek.

"Oh, nevermind," she said, brushing her hair with the back of her hand. Mary Jane couldn't be sure, but before she walked away, she thought she saw a tear glistening in her mother's eyes.

* * *

Later that afternoon she finally got a chance to hang out with Wendy, if only for a couple of hours. It was Mary Jane who had called her up and asked if there was any chance they could get together. And the only time Wendy could slip her into an over-packed schedule was between play practice and dinner.

"I've just been so busy with the show and everything," Wendy said apologetically as she let Mary Jane through the front door.

"I know, it's cool. We can hear you guys rehearsing. You sound amazing."

"Do I? Really?" Wendy grinned.

Mary Jane had meant that everyone sounded amazing, which was true. But in reality, Wendy had sounded the most amazing. "Absolutely. Really, at one point we all thought you all were listening to the movie soundtrack, but it was really you."

What she failed to add was that the entire chorus realized it wasn't the soundtrack the moment Bernie Glick chimed in. At that point the sounds from the next room went from Broadway belter to nasal whiner.

"That's so great! Oh, and we hear the chorus is doing fantastic stuff as well."

Mary Jane wasn't sure how to respond, so she decided to go for the truth. "Yeah, well. Not really. Ms. Krumplesteater has us walking around in circles. The only way to tell the ballroom scene from the Covent Garden dance is because in one, we walk clockwise. The other, counter-clockwise. Go team."

"Oh. But don't you have a special part? I mean, that's what Bernie said."

Ah yes. Bernie Glick, the Oracle of All Things. "A special part in the chorus? Sure. I'm the Elderly Duchess with Quizzing Glass at the ball, High Kicking Girl in Rags in Covent Garden, and, of course, the memorable Lisping Snob at the racetrack."

"You don't have to get mean," Wendy mumbled.

"I'm not getting mean, really! It's just that you're so good, and that's fantastic. But I feel sort of wasted here. I've had almost ten years of ballet training, and it's not as if any one of five hundred kids at Midtown couldn't be walking clockwise to a volleyball coach's whistle just the same as I am. If you hadn't made me promise...I don't know," she shrugged.

"*Made you promise?*" For a long moment Wendy was silent. Then she looked up. "You're just ticked off because someone else is the star."

Mary Jane's jaw literally dropped. "That's so not true!" But something about the accusation bothered her, some nudging truth behind those words that she chose to ignore for the time being.

"It *is* true. Let's face it, you were the star ballet dancer, the star cheerleader. You never had time for me, because you were always running off to the city for your precious ballet lessons, or your all-important rah-rah rehearsals. Then you dated the star jock Peter, before he returned to his usual place in the background. And you had Harry Osborn go after you – back when he was the coolest guy at Midtown. Then you and Peter dropped him like a bad habit after his dad got busted. "Now you're just in the chorus, just a face in the crowd. It must be killing you not to be onstage, front and center. Pretty, perfect Mary Jane. It must be really killing you that I'm the star now. Me. Funny Wendy, everyone's pal. The good sport. The chunky girl."

As she spoke, Wendy's face got redder, and her voice rose to a higher pitch than Mary Jane had ever heard.

"And I see the look on your face when I mention Bernie. He's not cool enough, is he? And you probably think the only reason he likes me is because we're in the play together. But it's different. Because he's always liked me. The whole reason he tried out for the play was so that he could get up enough nerve to ask me out."

"That's wonderful," Mary Jane's own voice came out as a hollow rasp. "Bernie's a great guy. I'm so happy for you. And I'm so pleased you're Eliza."

Wendy continued as if Mary Jane hadn't spoken a word.

"I saw the look on your face when you read the cast list. You can't pretend you weren't shocked, girlfriend. You were beyond shock. You were in total denial. You never knew what hit you."

"Wendy, I..."

"And you know what? I saw Peter talking to the newly cool Gwen Stacy. But this time I didn't notice him looking around for you the way he always does. He was happy just to be chatting it up with Gwen. No one remembers who made her look so hot, you know. No one cares that you were her fairy godmother with your mother's cheesy makeup."

Mary Jane couldn't breathe for a moment. The entrance to Wendy's house seemed to be spinning.

"I..." Wendy clamped her hand over her own mouth. "Mary Jane, I don't know what's wrong with me! I so didn't mean any of that!"

"Yes, you did," Mary Jane whispered. She felt hollow, empty. A big nothingness where her emotions should be. And very, very surprised.

Had she been treating Wendy like that all along? Was it possible that she hadn't even realized how unintentionally cruel she had been? That was totally unlike her. But then, everything had been so different the past few months. Everything had changed. So who could tell who the real Mary Jane actually was?

Suddenly she couldn't see anything. The tears, heavy and stinging, fell hotly on her cheeks.

"Mary Jane, I..."

But Mary Jane couldn't speak. Even if she could, she had nothing to say, not really.

How can you speak when your insides have just been punched out?

All she could do was turn and walk away. Then the walk became a run. She thought she heard Wendy calling her name, but she wasn't sure.

Only one thing was certain. She had to get away. And she knew that no matter how much distance she tried to put between herself and what just happened, it would stay with her for a long, long time.

* * *

Mary Jane didn't bother waiting for Peter to call that night. She wasn't ready to talk about her fight with Wendy, but she desperately wanted to hear a friendly voice. He picked up on the first ring. "Hey, MJ! I was just about to call you. What's up with Harry?"

"What do you mean?" Mary Jane was taken aback. This wasn't how she expected to start the conversation.

"He's really upset. Said that you and I had promised to do something with him Saturday night, and that we stood him up."

"That's odd. Why would he —" And then, with a horrible thud of realization, she remembered. "Oh, no." All she could think of was the terrible things Wendy had said. That she had ignored some friends. That maybe she hadn't been such a good person after all.

"I, uh, told Harry last week we'd do something with him on Saturday. And then he reminded me when I was coming out of that horrible physics test and I was too caught up in my own drama to remember."

"Mary Jane. The poor guy really wigged out, and spent the evening hanging out with those creepy freshmen. Listen, I've gotta go. I need to call Harry to see if he's okay."

"Tell him it's all my fault, Peter. Really. I feel terrible about this." Maybe she really was selfish and egotistical.

"Don't worry." She could tell from his voice he was smiling.

"I'll make sure you get assigned full blame. I'll also add global warming and the plague for good measure."

At that she finally smiled. "Thanks, you're swell."

"I know. Good night, MJ."

"Good night, Pete." She stayed on, waiting for the soft click as he hung up. Then she replaced the receiver.

She only had one more bit of homework to do before going to bed, a few things she needed to check out online. She logged on, scanning her homework page. And then she heard the telltale blip of an Instant Message.

She couldn't believe it. It was HopCop54 again!

Hello, cutie-pie! I miss your sugar lips.

"Eww," she squealed as she quickly typed "Drop dead, creep!"

There was silence for a few minutes, and Mary Jane returned to her homework. And then...

Are you mad at me, Maddy?

Maddy. Madeline. MADELINE!

"You've GOT to be kidding me!" MJ said aloud. HotCop54 was emailing her mother! They shared the same stupid screen name on the account, since an extra name would be an extra five bucks.

"Yes," she typed. "I'm very, very angry. Please don't email me ever again, DogBreath."

Almost immediately, HotCop54 logged off. And hopefully, that would be the end of DogBreath, whoever he was.

Mary Jane made two vows. One, she would make an effort to be less self-absorbed. She had good friends, and she didn't want to lose them. And two, that no matter what, she would fork over five dollars to her mother to add her own screen name. Even though she didn't know who the heck HotCop54 was, she'd already been force-fed way too much information about the creep.

* * *

Harry Osborn didn't feel comfortable with the guys. A few months ago, he wouldn't have bothered glancing at his Rolex to give them the time of day. He would have been hanging out with some hot cheerleader, or that gymnastics chick, what's-her-name.

These guys were freshmen, for pity's sake. He hadn't been hanging out with freshmen since he was one himself, and then only if he had nothing better to do.

"Osborn," Tick snapped. "You're with us, right?"

Tick was the undisputed leader of this gang of mini-mites. He was a short, slight kid, with a maroon-colored buzz cut. As usual, he was wearing army pants and an over-sized camouflage jacket, as if a member of some discount military unit.

"Sure, I'm with you." Harry wondered what Peter and Mary Jane were doing right now. Even that annoying Wendy was better than this.

"Okay, what we need you to do is to drive the car."

"What car?"

One of the other kids, Alfie, giggled, and Tick shut him up. "The car we open up for you."

Harry shrugged. "I don't get it."

"I'll explain. See that car over there?"

Harry looked in the direction Tick was pointing. "The red Toyota?"

"Yes, the red Toyota. We will open the window and get the car started if you can drive it to this address in Brooklyn."

Suddenly Harry wanted to be anywhere but here, with these guys.

"Why do you want me to do that?" He shoved his hands into his pockets, as if that would prevent him from getting more involved than he already was.

"Because that's how we get paid. It's very simple. That car is a few years old, right?"

Harry glanced at the car and nodded.

"As it is, it's worth a few thousand bucks. But if we take it to the chop shop, they take it apart and use the parts. And then the car is worth about twenty-five G's, and we get a cut."

"Twenty-five thousand dollars?" That sum used to be chump change to Harry. Now it seemed a staggering amount. He frowned. "Whose car is it?"

Tick shrugged. "Who knows? And who cares?" Although he was younger, something in his eyes made Harry uneasy.

"Hey, listen," Harry said quietly. "I don't want to get into any trouble." He thought of his dad, at that moment locked up in a maximum-security prison. The last thing he wanted was to join his dad in the Orange Jumpsuit Club.

"We won't get caught," Alfie said with certainty. "It will only take a few seconds to jack. And since you drive already, and look old enough, nobody is going to stop you. Once we get into Brooklyn, the car will vanish into a garage and come out in pieces. No one can ever trace this to us."

"What about the poor guy who owns the car?" Harry asked.

"The poor guy will be delighted!" Tick laughed. "He has insurance. And in a few days, he'll get a brand new set of wheels. This is what is known as a victimless crime, my friend."

"I don't know. It just doesn't seem right." A sinking feeling settled into Harry's stomach.

"Sorry, dude. We do this now, and it stays between us. Or else."

"Or else?" Harry smiled nervously at the melodramatic tone in Tick's voice, but he didn't smile back. The sinking feeling was replaced with a fluttering.

"Thanks for asking, but..."

And then, very casually, Tick pulled out a knife. It wasn't a particularly large knife, but it looked sharp. And it glinted menacingly under the streetlights. He stared at Harry, then very slowly, began to clean his fingernails with the tip. "Come on, Harry. Just this once?"

Harry looked at the other guys. There were only three of them. And they all looked more than a little frightened.

"I don't think so," Harry said, swallowing hard.

"You'll be back at home in an hour, with a couple hundred bucks in your pocket. Doesn't that sound good? And we won't get caught. Promise." He touched the tip of the blade with his finger, then drew it back. "Ouch," he said softly.

"Well..." He wished more than anything he could call his father, or Peter. Or anyone. But who would return his call?

Tick was right. Harry was home in an hour, not with a couple of hundred dollars, but seventy. He balled up the dollars and stuck them in his sock drawer. Part of him didn't want to use that money. No matter what he bought with it, he would be reminded of how the money came to him. Of the dirty garage, the even dirtier man working there. He would always know where that seventy dollars came from.

There was a message for him. Peter had called, and asked him to call back right away, no matter how late.

It was a call Harry did not return.

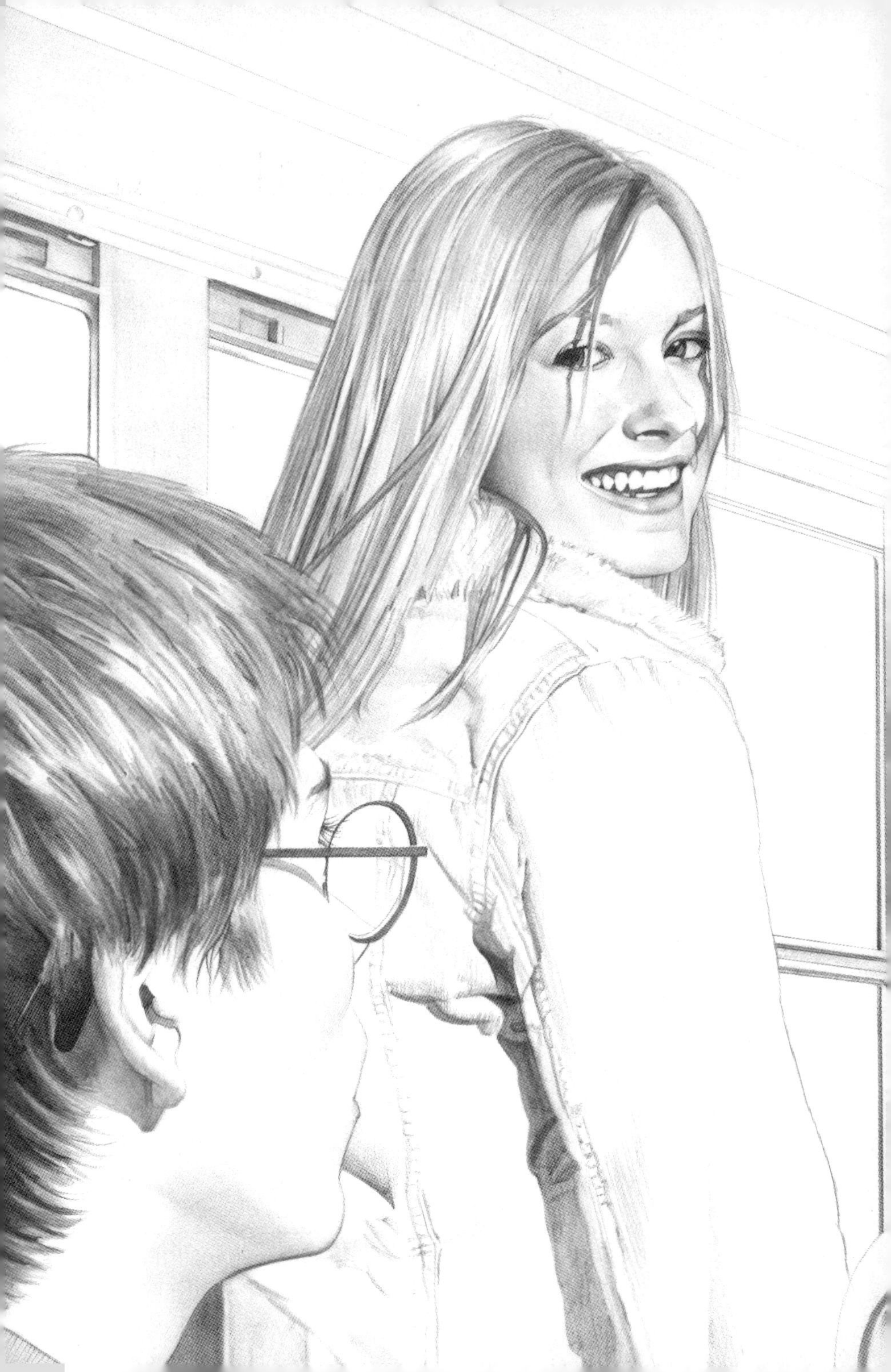

chapter 6

Like some old movie, with the bold-letter calendar pages of the day peeling off with invisible hands, the date of the Winter Formal finally arrived.

There was an electricity in the air the whole week before. Rehearsals were cut short for the play, and athletic practices were lighter than usual. Kids gathered in clusters, the guys discussing how dorky they were all going to look in the rented tuxes, yet all secretly pleased. The girls described their gowns to each other in the rabid hopes that no one else had the same dress, or even a similar dress.

A lot of them didn't have dates, which was perfectly okay, since a bunch of kids were attending the dance in groups. Of course, there were the theater kids, who always made a big deal of dancing together in the center of the floor. There were the jocks, who hung around the sides and made comments about people as they passed. And the smart kids, who would spend the evening talking about college applications and who was likely to win the school essay contest.

Most of the kids had already decided who they would like to hook up with at the dance, but pretended to be totally open to anyone who seemed agreeable. Or at least to the first person who expressed any interest in them. In short, everyone was psyched.

Even the teachers all made comments, assigning little or no homework and warning everyone to be careful, to drive responsibly. During the last period of the day, the principal made an announcement on the intercom system, again repeating the same old "safety first" routine.

It had been such an odd day, almost surreal. Everyone was going through the motions of attending classes, but really their minds could not be further from American History or Physics. It was as if the entire school had been holding its collective breath in anticipation of the dance.

But for Mary Jane, a long shadow had been cast over the event. Every time she would get excited about the dance, the vague unease over Wendy would nudge into her thoughts. They'd seen each other since the afternoon of the argument, of course. There was school and lunch and rehearsal for the musical. But neither mentioned what had been said that day. It was as if an unspoken agreement existed that they would not talk about it until they were ready. And at the moment, they were definitely not ready. Mary Jane desperately wanted to discuss it, but at the same time, hoped it would just go away on its own.

The day itself, Mary Jane and Wendy got together for the special beautification rites, which included manicures and pedicures, exploring the whole new line of Skye Bleu products, and experimenting with different, but not daring, hair styles.

Of course, there was no thought of perming or straightening, of highlighting or coloring their hair. Not at this late date. That would be all but begging for disaster. And everyone knew the cautionary tale of some senior in a neighboring school district who decided to go blonde the day of her senior dance, and ending up going bald instead.

It was odd to go through the usual rituals with Wendy, but not be totally at ease. Their conversation was safe and light, nothing personal. No hints of anything darker than misapplied mascara. Both were reluctant to mention their dates, since that fell into the potentially dangerous, might-lead-to-something-personal category. Bernie and Peter's names were not even brought up. So instead they concentrated strictly on the safe topic of getting ready for the dance. Mary Jane had even briefly thought of inviting Gwen Stacy to come over, but then decided she might feel weird having someone she didn't know that well watching her and Wendy at their most vulnerable. As if the unspoken strain between them wasn't weird enough already.

In spite of their surface excitement, there was also another uncertainty they both refused to acknowledge. What if the dance was a disaster? What if they fell into the sound equipment, or came out of the ladies' room trailing toilet paper on their high heels? Or laughed enchantingly, only to discover later they had enormous boogers hanging out of their noses? Or the seams of their gowns suddenly gave way in the middle of twirling on the dance floor?

Above all, they were both worried that the uncomfortable and uneasy peace between them would somehow explode and ruin everything, not only the dance, but their friendship. Their conversation was light, safe, completely polite — and not nearly enough fun.

Wendy paused as she contemplated her hair. "Up or down?"

Mary Jane flipped open a fashion magazine. "Well, according to the experts, hair in an upswept style is considered a little dressier. For those red carpet moments, you know."

"I'm not going to the Oscars. I'm going to the Winter Formal." She held her hair back. "I have no neck."

"Excuse me?"

"Seriously. I have no neck. That's why I never wear my hair in a ponytail. My head sits directly on my shoulders. See?" Wendy turned to Mary Jane.

"That's not true," Mary Jane slid off her bed. "Maybe some tendrils."

"Tendrils?"

"Like in romance novels. You know, their exquisite faces are always framed with equally exquisite tendrils."

Mary Jane, an expert in putting hair up after all those years of ballet, scrutinized her friend's hair, and within moments had arranged the glossy dark curls into a elegant French twist surrounded by a cascade of tendrils.

"Wow," Wendy smiled, afraid to admit how great her hair looked, just in case it really didn't and she was simply hoping it looked that good.

"Okay, I'll admit it. You look fantastic!"

Madeline Watson knocked gently on the door. "Hey, girls. It's after five-thirty, and you might want to wrap things up if you're going to make it to dinner."

"Five-thirty!" Mary Jane and Wendy looked at each other.

"I've gotta get home," Wendy began gathering her things. "We're all meeting at the Italian Villa in an hour."

"I love that place," Mary Jane helped her zip a few things into her backpack. "They have great lasagna."

"Yeah, I know. Where are you and Peter going?"

This was the first time all afternoon a guy's name was mentioned, other than Ralph Lauren or Max Factor.

"He won't tell me. He says it's a big surprise," she laughed. "So I suspect we'll be the next table over at the Italian Villa."

"Really?" Wendy didn't seem exactly thrilled at the thought.

"Nah." She tried not to appear hurt. "Maybe we'll be at Hot Dog King. Two dogs for a dollar."

"Cool. We'll, I'm out of here. See you at the dance!"

They gave each other the traditional socialite air kiss, so as not to smudge their carefully finished makeup, and wished each other a wonderful time. It was almost as if they weren't going to the same place at all, or if they were, that they wouldn't see each other. Mary Jane watched her friend walk away, wondering if that strange, invisible wall would ever go away.

* * *

"Oh, Mary Jane! You look beautiful, absolutely beautiful!" Her mother clasped her hands together, her eyes glistening with tears, and watched Mary Jane pace back and forth in the living room.

"You have to say that," she said looking up at the clock for the third time in a minute. "It's required of all parents."

What if Peter was late? What if he decided this whole thing was too much trouble, that renting a tux and everything else would be too expensive? She knew that since Uncle Ben's death, Peter and his Aunt May had been living pretty close to the edge financially. There was some money coming in from Uncle Ben's insurance, and from Social Security or something like that. But she knew it wasn't very much. So she wouldn't blame him if he just bagged the whole thing.

"Mary Jane, that gown is stunning on you, and the color is, well, perfect. And the pearls. And what you've done with your hair. You have never been more exquisite."

On second thought, she *would* blame Peter if he just bagged the whole thing. How rude! Here she was all dressed up, all ready to go to some mystery place before the dance and...

The downstairs bell rang.

He was here.

Mary Jane took a deep breath as her mom buzzed him up. She faced the mirror one last time, critically appraising the end result. And she had to admit, she did look pretty good.

Really, most of that was due to the dress her mother had made. It was completely gorgeous, even better than the one in the magazine. And since her mother had made it, they were able to make a few adjustments, like taking in the bustle-like folds in the back, and crossing the straps in the back for an extra bit of detail.

She was glad she went with the upswept hair, she concluded. It did look a lot dressier, and her mother had found a small silk flower to pin at the side. She wore the restrung pearls with matching pearl earrings. Well, okay. So the earrings were from the drugstore and were genuine plastic. Maybe if she moved her head around enough, nobody would notice.

Peter would be there in a moment in his rented tux. And suddenly she had a terrible, traitorous thought: What if he rented one of those powder blue things, with a matching ruffled shirt and bow tie?

Great. Then all he'd need was an accordion around his neck to complete the picture.

She knew he probably waited until the last minute to reserve it. Mary Jane bet most of the guys had picked theirs out months ago, even before they had picked out their dates. That would be just like Peter, too. Cute as he was, he was completely oblivious to fashion. Even to color. Which would explain his attachment to that red and green striped tee shirt, which made him look like one of Santa's more demented helpers. Or the brown cargo shorts with the big rip in the seat.

He knocked on the door twice.

Madeline Watson gave a girlish giggle and opened the door.

"Hi, Mrs. Watson. I..."

Peter's voice trailed off as he looked at Mary Jane, his eyes almost comically wide. And then his cheeks and ears flushed red. "Wow," his voice cracked. "I mean, Mary Jane."

He couldn't even blink, as if not willing to miss a single instant of her. All he could do was stare at how amazingly beautiful she looked, like some sort of movie star. For him, it was hard to take in the details, of the gown, of her hair. They all blurred together. All he saw clearly was a vision in green satin, or something, and her auburn hair pulled off her face.

But it was her face that left him speechless. She seemed to radiate a kind of inner beauty that was suddenly showing itself on the outside. This was how he had always envisioned her in his mind. Now everyone would see her, really see her as she truly was.

"Wow," he said again, his mouth suddenly dry.

Mary Jane stared at Peter as well, no less stunned. He looked awesome! Instead of one of those pastel bridal party tuxedos, his was plain black, with subtle black lapels and matching cummerbund. Underneath he wore a crisp white shirt with tiny pleats instead of ruffles.

"Is that a real tie?"

He seemed surprised that she spoke. He'd been so mesmerized, he had temporarily forgotten where he was and what they were doing. And he'd certainly forgotten all about the tie.

"This?" He reached up and touched it, then grinned. "Oh, yeah. That's why I'm a little late. It is real, but I'd never tied one of these things before. Aunt May finally had to bail me out."

"You look fantastic, Peter." And he did, he really did. Even his hair, slightly shaggy and occasionally unruly, was combed back.

"Thanks." He seemed embarrassed. "This was Uncle Ben's. Seems he last wore it in 1953."

"I hear that was a good year for tuxedos."

They stood for a moment, just happy to be there, smiling and staring at each other.

Madeline Watson cleared her throat and gestured towards the clear plastic box he was clutching. "Peter? Is that for Mary Jane?"

"Cripes! I almost forgot!" He shoved the box in Mary Jane's direction. "It's a corsage. I couldn't remember what color your dress was going to be, so this is just plain white. Well, mostly white anyway. Is that okay?"

"It's beautiful," she said. And it was, a single delicate orchid tinted with just the faintest hint of pink.

"And it can go anywhere. I mean, it can be for your wrist or for your, um." He motioned vaguely at his shoulders. "Wherever."

"How lovely, Peter," Madeline helped Mary Jane open the box. "What do you think, on your wrist?"

Mary Jane had the distinct impression that her mother was biting the inside of her cheek to keep from laughing. "Sure. The wrist would be great."

Peter watched intently as she slipped the corsage on her left wrist. "Thank you," she said softly.

He simply beamed.

"Well," he said at last. "I guess we should get going."

"Not without pictures, you don't!" Madeline pulled out her camera, and both Peter and Mary Jane groaned.

But then they looked at each other, and were suddenly very glad they would have photos to remember the night with.

After a few poses, Peter held out his arm. "Shall we?" Madeline placed the matching wrap she had made around her daughter's shoulders. "Have fun, honey. And don't forget I put an extra twenty dollars in your purse." With that she kissed her on the forehead.

Then Mary Jane slipped her hand through the crook of his arm, her purse in her other hand. "We shall."

And off they went.

* * *

Peter helped her out of the taxi cab, taking her hand as if she was a royal princess descending from a carriage.

"Yo. Eighteen bucks," said the driver. He flicked the pine-scented air freshener on his rearview mirror. It was made in the shape of a Christmas tree, but somehow smelled more like cherry soda mixed with coconut tanning lotion.

They were in Manhattan's Upper East Side, nowhere near the Italian Villa in Queens. Peter peeled off the bills and paid the driver, who stepped on the gas, narrowly missing a woman with shopping bags who was hailing a cab.

Peter watched the cab weave in and out of the traffic. "What a creep," he muttered.

"So where are we going?" Mary Jane held the wrap close. It was cold out, and the flimsy bit of cloth really didn't do much to keep her warm.

Peter just kept staring at the back of the cab. "Really, someone should stop that guy. He could have killed that lady with the bags."

"I'm freezing," Mary Jane said simply.

"Oh, I'm sorry!" Suddenly he was attentive again, all thoughts of the reckless cab driver gone. Then he looked incredibly pleased. "*Voila*, Madame."

Mary Jane blinked, then realized he was motioning to a brownstone townhouse with tiny white lights all over the front hedges. A small sign, subtle but beautifully painted, was placed discreetly by the front door. Mary Jane gasped when she read it. "Le Petite Araignee! You're kidding, right?"

"Nope. Harry suggested it. Said it was a great place for a special occasion."

"Yeah, like a coronation." A doorman in a crisp red uniform appeared, beckoning them with a welcoming gesture. "Really, Peter. I appreciate this and everything, but it's too much."

He looked slightly crestfallen. "What do you mean?"

"This place is incredibly expensive."

"Harry said it was really quite reasonable. Besides, I've been saving up. I'm completely prepared."

"But Peter, between the corsage and the dance tickets themselves, which I know were twenty dollars a piece, and the cab and..."

"And think of what I saved by not having to rent a tux," he said, brushing his lapels. "Seriously, Mary Jane, the tux is by far the biggest expense. I know what I'm doing." Then he tilted his head slightly. "Why, don't you trust me?"

"Of course I do! It's just that..."

"Shush," he said, placing a finger on her lips. "I know what I'm doing. Let's just eat. I'm starving."

"Okay," she said with less conviction than she had meant to. It seemed like such a waste. But on the other hand, if this was really what he wanted, well. Maybe she shouldn't be such a wet blanket. Then she smiled. "Why not?"

The doorman held the door wide, and Peter and Mary Jane entered what seemed to be a fantasy world. Another person, this one in a black tuxedo — clearly not rented — met them at a wooden podium.

"*Bon soir,*" he smiled. "Your name?"

"Peter," his voice broke. Then he cleared his throat and spoke again. "Mr. Peter Parker."

The man raised his eyebrows and looked down a long piece of paper, his finger scrolling past the names. "Ah," he said with triumph. Then he marked off their names and motioned towards yet a third uniformed man.

Uniformed Man Number Three looked as if he belonged on some luxury liner from days gone by, in a white fitted suit with twinkling brass buttons and a military collar. Mary Jane had a brief, unwelcome image of the Titanic, but decided to ignore it.

Everything was hushed and subdued, the quiet tinkle of glasses, the gentle hum of conversation. It was one of those places where you instinctively whispered, where a single "How ya doin'?" would be as out of place as asking the Queen of England what she carried in those big old ugly handbags. She couldn't help but notice that some of the other diners, seated at large tables with more silver, china and glassware than seemed entirely necessary, smiled at them as they were led to their table.

The decor was undeniably beautiful, in a Buckingham Palace sort of way. It was almost like walking into a museum. The chairs looked stiff; everything was ironed and pressed. Nothing was out of place, not a single, gold-framed painting was even slightly crooked. The flowers, arranged in strategically placed vases, looked as if they had been molded rather than grown. Even the butter next to the rolls was shaped into perfect, artful curls, too pretty to smear all over a piece of bread. The whole place gave Mary Jane the impression of a very well-dressed person who needed to have their hair ruffled. Badly.

They arrived at the table, one of the smallest in the room. Mary Jane was pleased. Maybe the smaller the table, the cheaper the meal.

Both Peter and the man in the white uniform began to pull out a chair for her, and for a moment both refused to let go of the chair's back. Finally Peter outstared him. He shrugged an apology and let Peter do the honors. As they settled into their seats, every bit as uncomfortable as she suspected, they were handed oversized menus covered in padded leather.

"It's like the Gutenberg bible," he whispered.

"Only a little heavier," she answered over the top of the thing.

Yet another man in a uniform, this one in red with a silver cup on a silver chain around his neck, stopped by the table. He stood for a moment, then did a half-bow and — did he click his heels? — left.

Peter gave a half-smile. "The sommelier. Guess he figured we were too young to drink wine."

"That's a relief. I thought for a moment he was the head jailer of the dungeon."

They both laughed, and immediately hushed themselves as other patrons turned their silver coifed heads and watched.

Mary Jane began the serious task of checking out the menu. At first she was confused, since there were no prices. Just lots of food with French-sounding names listed and, luckily, English translations in small print below. Then she figured it out. This was one of those prix fixe places. No matter what they ordered, it was all the same price.

Peter was frowning at his own menu. "Don't worry," she said quietly. "The translations in English are right below."

"Yeah. I see." He still didn't look too happy.

But Mary Jane knew exactly why. The food was as pretentious-sounding as the place looked. Poor guy. They probably would have been better off at Hot Dog King.

She actually remembered eating at places like this when she was little, when her family still lived in a big Park Avenue penthouse. When they had lots of money and she went to private schools and had horseback riding and tennis lessons. When her dad still lived with them. Unconsciously she fingered the pearls, the wedding gift her father had given her mother so long ago.

"Those are really pretty," Peter said.

"Thanks," she flashed a smile. Then her eyes widened. "They have Dover sole!"

"Excuse me?"

"My dad used to order it all the time. See? Under the seafood section. Flown in fresh daily from England. You know, the White Cliffs of Dover."

"Yep. With a first-class ticket," he muttered to himself.

"*Pardonez-moi?*" She asked, getting into the spirit of the place.

"Nothing."

"That's what I'm having, the Dover sole, with white asparagus and a truffle salad. What do you want?"

Peter shook his head. "I don't know. Maybe just a salad. Or some soup."

Her heart went out to him. He must have felt so uncomfortable there, with all the French foods, all the waiters. Funny, it was coming back to her now, how it felt to be in a restaurant like Le Petite Araignee. She touched his leg with her foot under the table.

"Geez!" He almost jumped three feet. "What the...oh. That's your foot. Sorry, I thought it was a cat or something."

Mary Jane shook her head and relaxed, really relaxed for the first time that evening. She was so lucky! Here she was with Peter, the most wonderful guy in the world. Well, in any case, the most wonderful guy in her world. And he was looking sensational in that glorious tuxedo.

"You really look amazing," she said softly.

He looked up, slightly surprised. "Oh, thanks."

This was where she belonged. Here, on the Upper East Side. At Le Petite Araignee with Peter Parker. "You know, the Bradford School is just around the corner."

Peter had attended the private school until his parents died, and Mary Jane until the Watson bank account suffered a similar fate. The last time they were here in this neighborhood together, they were little kids and science project partners; now they were sharing their first fancy date.

"Yeah, I know. Wonder if they had fish sticks today." Then, oddly, he added, "Dover sole sticks."

At last a brand new man in uniform, this one dressed as a military aid-de-camp, came by the table. "*Bon soir.* Are you ready to order?"

He turned to Mary Jane first, a questioning smile on his face. Something about that smile annoyed her. It was slightly condescending. Didn't he realize she used to go to places like this all the time? That she was accustomed to white linen tablecloths and napkins, that she knew exactly which fork to use with what?

She pursed her lips and looked at the menu. "I'll start out with the soup, excuse me, the *potage de Bordeaux*, then the lobster brioche. Next, the Dover sole with white asparagus and truffles. Oh, and to begin with, may we share *les petites pates a la Anglaise?*" She closed her menu with satisfaction.

Peter's eyes were wide. And was that a sheen of perspiration appearing on his upper lip?

Then he shrugged. "Oh, what the heck. I'll have the filet mignon and a salad."

The waiter leaned forward helpfully. "And perhaps the *pommes de terre a la royal?*"

"Sure. What's a steak without a potato, eh?"

"And to drink, Monsieur?"

"Mary Jane?" Peter held out his hand. "What would you like, *un petite* Coke?"

She nodded. "Make that two," he said. "Excuse me. *Deux.*"

The waiter seemed to sneer for a brief moment, then it went away. And so did he with their order and the bulky menus.

"Well," she leaned back in her chair. "This is really a great place, Peter. Thank you."

"You're welcome. I figured, well." He reached across the small table, knocking over the silver salt dish. "Whoops." Quickly he scraped the salt up with a knife and began putting it back into the dish. But before he could do it, another guy in a uniform was at the table with a fresh dish.

Wordlessly, the younger waiter, clearly a private, as he had no ribbons or brass buttons, removed the empty one.

"Thanks," Peter said.

The young waiter smiled. "No problem," he said before he went back to his post.

"Wow. He's about our age," Peter wondered.

But all Mary Jane could do was look at Peter. Suddenly she wanted to ask him something, something she'd been meaning to ask him for weeks now. But they just never seemed to get a chance. "Peter, how are you doing?"

He looked away from the young waiter. "Fine. Other than being a total klutz. I mean really, they should have covers on those salt thingies. It's unhygienic. A guy could sneeze all over the table and..."

"No, really. How are you?" Now she reached over the table. And after a moment, he sighed and reached to hold her hand. He seemed reluctant to speak, and watched his own thumb as he rubbed it in small circles over the top of her hand. "I don't know, Mary Jane. Sometimes I wake up in the middle of the night and still thing it was all a dream, all a nightmare."

"Uncle Ben."

"Uncle Ben. Harry and his dad. Getting bitten by that spider."

"I thought your hand was all better. Does it still hurt?" She turned his hand over and held it towards the candle. There was a small circular scar, a slightly discolored purplish gray.

"No, it doesn't hurt," he flipped his hand back over. "It's just that, well. I've really changed."

She looked at him, really looked hard. And he did seem different. There were circles under his eyes that hadn't been there before, a weariness that was strangely compelling.

"It must be so hard without Uncle Ben."

"It is," he swallowed. "Everything in that house reminds me of him, reminds me that he's gone. It takes me by surprise. I'll be thinking about something else, about a test at school or what I'm in the mood to eat. And suddenly, out of nowhere, I see the mark on the wall where he tried to hang that silly matador painting he did last year in his art class. Or the duct tape around the kitchen faucet. Stuff like that."

"He loved you very much, you know. It was obvious when he looked at you, how he loved you. How proud he was of you."

"Yeah, and in return I was such a total jerk."

"No, you weren't. You were a kid."

He shrugged, and she continued. "How is Aunt May?"

"Aunt May." Again he swallowed. "Sometimes I hear her crying at night. I don't go to her, because then she'll stop crying, and I think she needs to cry. Is it weird of me to think that?"

Mary Jane shook her head slowly. "Not at all. I mean, how can you ever get over a loss like that?"

"I don't think you do. And then, well..."

"What, Peter?"

"I caught her crying over the electric bill. I mean, it was pretty high. But when Uncle Ben was around, she used to get ticked off at the electric bill and the gas and all that. I try to give her what I can, you know. From odd jobs. Hopefully I'll sell a few photos someplace, and that might cover a few things. Keep her from crying over a bill now and then. That," he cleared his throat. "That would be good."

"Oh, Peter." Mary Jane wasn't sure if there was anything she could say, anything at all that might make things even a little better. "What can I do?"

Then he smiled slightly. "Just keep on being you. Keep on being my friend." He glanced down. "My girlfriend."

She felt a flutter in her stomach, not at all unpleasant. In fact, it was really nice to hear him call her his girlfriend.

"Enough about me." This time he had a genuine grin that lit up his eyes. "What's up with you? Have you and Wendy resolved things? I know she was over this afternoon, getting all dolled up with you."

"Things are weird with her, Pete. It's as if there's some sort of barrier between us. Has that ever happened to you?"

"Sure. It's happening right now with Harry. I keep on calling him, trying to get some sort of conversation going. And when I finally reach him, he just answers with 'yep' or 'nope.' Which even for Harry, is a little weird."

"I guess all we can do is keep trying with our friends, to not give up."

He nodded. Just then the young waiter guy came over. "*Deux* Cokes," he said, placing two glasses of soda before them. "Hey," he said under his breath to Peter. "Don't you go to Midtown?"

"Yeah. How did you know?" Peter spoke as softly as the waiter.

With ice tongs and a silver bucket, he dropped three cubes in each glass. "I saw you play basketball a few months ago. My cousin goes to Tech. Man, you guys really kicked their..."

Suddenly a more senior military man returned and glared, and the younger waiter vanished.

"Hey, how's ballet going?" He sipped his soda.

Mary Jane shrugged and looked away.

Peter put down his glass. "Go on," he urged.

"I don't know. I really love it still, you know that."

"And you're really good at it."

"Thanks. But it's just so all-consuming. I mean, they expect dancers to give up so much for the chance of being in the company."

"I thought that's what you've always dreamed of, to become a ballerina with the Manhattan Ballet Company."

"I thought so, too. It's just that there's so much else I want to do. Why are you smiling?"

"Remember a few weeks ago, when I quit the basketball team for that very same reason?"

She reached over and squeezed his hand. "Point taken."

"Make that three points from downtown," he laughed.

And just then a veritable army of waiters appeared with trays and covered dishes, with oversized pepper mills and different silver serving spoons and forks and knives for each course.

The food was all right, she supposed. The lobster was nice, and the soup was cold, which she hadn't expected. She'd forgotten that pate was really just liverwurst. The fish was fine, although she couldn't tell the difference between the special Dover sole and the fillets her mother bought at the supermarket.

There was one awkward moment when the waiter asked Peter if he wanted ketchup with the steak, but Peter, showing great restraint, merely smiled and shook his head. At one point the nice younger waiter came over and slipped them some extra soda, which they both thought was sweet.

While they ate they noticed a network anchorman sitting in the corner. His hair looked suspiciously red and synthetic even under the dim lighting in the room. And on the other side was an actress Mary Jane had seen in some PBS production. She looked older in real life, and kept on glancing around at the other patrons, as if hoping someone, anyone, would recognize her, or ask for her autograph.

"It's really kind of sad," she said.

Peter nodded, finishing up his last bit of steak. "Well, as long as they don't know how sad they are, it's probably okay."

The moment he put down his fork, the main waiter reappeared with the dessert menu. "Sure, why not? It really doesn't matter anymore." Peter ordered chocolate mousse, and Mary Jane, after much indecision, ordered the same thing.

"I'll be right back," she said, folding her napkin. "The ladies' room," she whispered.

"I figured," he rose slightly as she stood up to leave, then settled back into his chair.

She found the ladies' room with no problem. But as she passed one of the patrons, she caught a glimpse of his menu. And his had the prices on them.

Boy, did his ever have prices!

She froze for a moment, scanning some of the numbers. The filet mignon was thirty-eight dollars! The soup she had was thirteen! And the fish, the Dover sole...

"Forty-three dollars!" She shouted. The patron startled, and she moved on.

"Excuse me," she said to the first waiter she found. "I think there's been some terrible mistake. My menu did not have the prices listed."

"But of course not," he smiled with the false compassion of an executioner. "The ladies never get the prices, only the gentlemen."

"That's not fair!"

"We seldom receive any complaints, Mademoiselle," he replied frostily.

She clamped her hand over her mouth to avoid whimpering.

The bathroom. She needed to splash some cold water on her face and think.

But offered no comfort. Only a woman in her own uniform and an apron who was there to hand her a towel...and take more money.

No wonder Peter had looked so uncomfortable. What a total jerk she had been! Why had she ordered all those dishes, the lobster. The fish.

"The truffles," she moaned.

And she had eaten them. There was no way to take back the merchandise.

One of the bathroom stalls opened just then, and a slender, elegant woman stepped over to the sink.

"Mary Jane? Little Mary Jane Watson? Is that you?"

Mary Jane stiffened. "Yes?" And through her panic she saw who it was. Mrs. Horton Stevens, Biffy to her friends, one of her grandmother's luncheon companions and now, one of her mother's very best Skye Bleu clients. "Oh, hello, Mrs. Stevens. How are you?"

"I'm fine, Mary Jane. Just fine. My, how pretty you're becoming." Then she peered closer. "Is that the new Skye Bleu New Horizon line?"

Mary Jane was stunned for a few seconds, wondering what Mrs. Stevens was talking about. Then she realized it was her makeup. "Oh, yes it is. My mother let me borrow some."

"Why, I love it! I do believe those shades would go just right with my complexion, don't you?"

"Um, sure. Yes, I do. They will be perfect." What was she going to do? She only had about thirty-five dollars in her purse, and that included her mother's emergency money.

"Is there anything wrong, dear?" Mrs. Stevens asked.

The bathroom attendant was listening, but trying to be discreet. Mary Jane didn't care.

"Oh, Mrs. Stevens. This is so terrible. I'm here on a date, a really nice guy. My boyfriend, actually. And I don't know how he can possibly have enough money to pay the bill."

Mrs. Stevens just stared at her. "Is that Fleure de Mauve?"

"Excuse me?"

"Your lipstick. Is that Fleure de Mauve? I saw it in the Spring Preview catalog, but it looks much better in real life."

"Yes, yes." Mary Jane opened her purse and handed her the lipstick. "Here, Mrs. Stevens. Take it. It will look great on you."

Mary Jane felt as if she was locked in some bizarre stage play, with absurd characters in ridiculous situations.

"Why, thank you, dear!" With great deliberation she applied the lipstick, then blotted her lips, leaving a great big pink stain on the linen towel. "Oh, I love it! Simply love it!"

Mary Jane nodded weakly. "I'm glad, Mrs. Stevens."

"Biffy. Please, call me Biffy." She was clearly delighted, and kept on staring at herself in the mirror. Then she looked again at Mary Jane. "Poor thing. Boyfriend's a little short on money?" Without saying another word she reached into her own purse, a silver-beaded number, and pulled out a wad of bills. "Here, honey. This should help."

"Mrs. Stevens!"

"Biffy! Call me Biffy!"

Although it wasn't easy, that's precisely what Mary Jane did. "Biffy! I can't possibly accept this!"

Biffy Stevens waved a hand, the jewels flashing under the fluorescent bathroom lights. "It's nothing. A loan, honey. I have an appointment to see your mother early next week, and she can pay me back then." Then she looked back at her reflection. "Oh, I just love this new shade!"

Mary Jane thought she would cry with gratitude. "Thank you, thank you so much." She thumbed through the bills. Four hundred dollars! She couldn't possibly use all that much money. She began to hand some of it back.

"No, Mary Jane. Keep it. This is Le Petite Araignee. Trust me, you'll need it." Then she pulled out another twenty and placed it in a gold dish on the marble sink. "This is for both of us," she said to the attendant, who smiled and nodded. Then she patted her hair and smiled one last time in the mirror. "Love this shade. I'll see you later, Mary Jane. And thank you again for the lipstick.'"

With that she waved and swept out of the ladies' room.

And Mary Jane sighed. Everything would be okay. She retouched her own makeup, and as she left she saw the attendant slip the twenty dollar bill into her apron.

* * *

Peter sat alone at the table, actual flop sweat now beginning to drip from his hairline.

He had just asked for the bill.

Mary Jane watched him as he opened his wallet, then closed it again. He ran his finger around the inside of his collar, as if loosening that would somehow help the situation.

After all he'd been through, the last thing he needed was to spend his prom night washing dishes in the kitchen of Le Petite Araignee. And after all the kind things he'd said and done, after all the wonderful things he had been to her, he wouldn't have to. She watched him from across the restaurant and smiled.

"Excuse me," she tapped their main waiter on his padded shoulder. "May I please have the bill?"

He stiffened. "I was just bringing it over to Monsieur," he said haughtily.

"Well, Mademoiselle wishes to take it, please."

His eyes narrowed, as if uncertain whether or not to trust someone who is not even trusted with the prices. Then he shrugged. "Certainly," and handed her the bill. Like the menu, it was in an embossed leather folder.

She wanted to pay it right away, before Mrs. Stevens left. That way she could give her the leftover change and...

The bill. Was it possible?

Four hundred and twenty-eight dollars!

She felt her knees buckle slightly, but she carefully placed Mrs. Stevens money, her own emergency twenty, and counted out eight singles before folding the leather back over.

Four hundred and twenty-eight dollars.

"Would you like any change, Mademoiselle?"

Did he sneer? She could have sworn he sneered. The whole place seemed to be one prolonged sneer.

"No, thank you," she said weakly, then walked carefully back to the table, not looking at a single item in her path. She didn't want to get charged for anything else.

Peter stood as she reached the table. "Mary Jane, I have to confess...Hey, are you all right?"

"Yeah, sure," she sat down and took a deep breath.

"Mary Jane, I have to...."

"Pay the tip."

"Huh?"

"I just paid the bill, so could you pay the tip?"

"How can you...could you...what do you mean?" He stammered.

"Please, let this be on me, Peter. Really. It's what I planned on all along."

"But you had no idea we were even going here! Remind me to kill Harry, by the way. 'Oh, it's very reasonable, Peter. Not expensive at all.' Yeah, sure."

"Peter, you're babbling."

"No, Mary Jane. I should pay. Please let me."

"Forget it, Peter. I just sold a lipstick. It's fine."

"Huh?

"Just let me pay."

Finally he agreed, reluctantly. Mary Jane didn't want him to know how expensive the meal had been.

He stopped and opened up his wallet. "How much should I leave?" He pulled out a twenty.

"A little more," she said.

Then another twenty. "More."

"A ten?"

"Ah, never mind. That should be enough," she said. "It's not as if we'll ever come back again."

"Whew," he closed his wallet. "I have just over ten bucks left. Mind if we take the subway to the dance?"

"I thought you'd never ask."

"Whew," he said again as he held her chair. "Wait a moment. I think I have to go to the mens' room."

She clamped her hand on his arm. "Can you possibly wait until we get to the dance?"

"Sure, I suppose so. Why?"

"Because trust me, Peter. We can't afford for you to go to the bathroom here."

He wasn't sure why, but he laughed. They both did. And as they headed towards the subway, their main waiter picked up his tip. It's wasn't nearly enough for the size of the bill.

He should have known it, a couple of kids.

This time, there was absolutely no mistaking it. He did sneer.

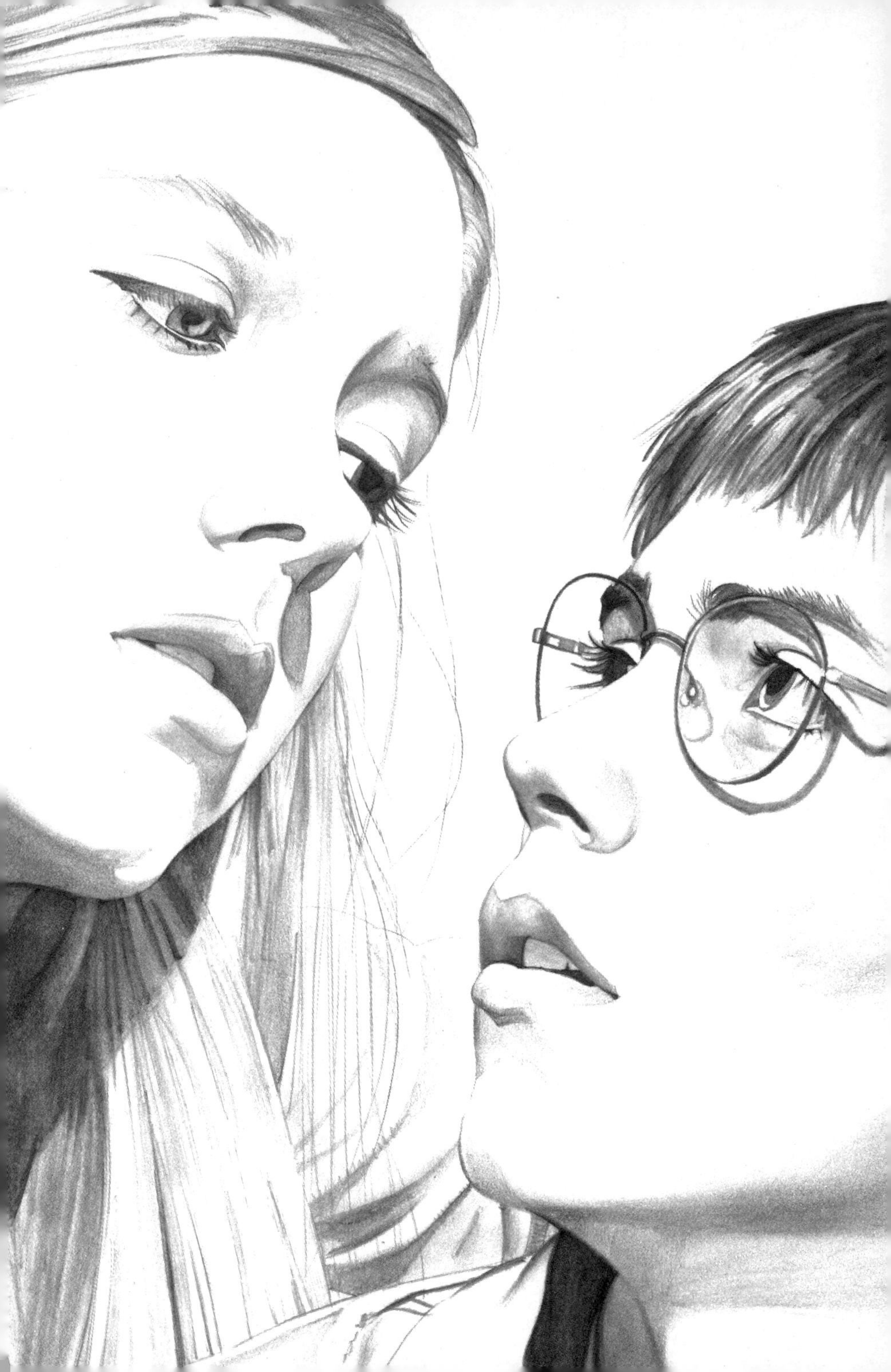

chapter 7

The theme for the Winter Formal was "An Icy Wonderland," perhaps not terribly original for an event held in December, but quite prudent when taking into account the three dozen large boxes of foil icicles left over from last year's student production "Nanook of the North." And the amount they saved in decorations was then earmarked for the entertainment.

On this topic, the first and most obvious decision was whether to go for a live band or for a disc jockey. The decision was made early on to go for a DJ. And luckily for Midtown, the president of the dance committee's older brother was a DJ whose career was just starting to take off. The place was vibrating with deafening, booming music. A mere eight hours earlier the gymnasium floor had been the scene of a fierce floor hockey match. But now the kids danced, swayed, and gyrated on it, some laughing, others shouting to each other — all in pantomime since the blasting sounds eliminated any chance of hearing non-amplified voices.

On the sides, the non-dancers watched the dancers, clustered in groups and shouting into each others ears about who was dancing with whom, whose gown looked the best, who had the funniest-looking tuxedo. Did Missy look fat in that tight dress? Was that an orange tux on that kid from Advanced Chemistry?

Was Mr. Rafferty, a science teacher and one of the chaperones, really wearing a tie imprinted with little yellow smiley faces?

In the middle of a sea of dancing, twirling bodies, Mary Jane and Peter attempted a conversation as they danced.

"Hey, look over there. Harry's dancing with Gwen Stacy."

Mary Jane turned her head in the direction he was pointing. "Oh, look at Gwen! What a fantastic dress. Harry looks happy."

"What?"

"I said, Harry looks happy," she shouted.

Peter looked around. "Who's Cathy?"

"Huh?"

Then Peter cupped his hands and yelled "Gwen looks hot!" Just as the song ended. A few people around them laughed.

Mary Jane wasn't one of them.

"Well," he said in a softer voice. "What I meant to say is that I can't feel too sorry for Harry. I didn't know he'd asked her. And at least those freshmen dweebs he's been hanging out with can't come to the upperclass dances. Anyway, Gwen sure looks great."

"I noticed," Mary Jane tried to keep her tone light.

Peter's eyes remained on the other couple, or on Gwen, for a little longer than Mary Jane felt altogether necessary.

"Hey," she said quickly, "Wendy told me that Gwen got poison ivy, like, four times last semester."

Peter chuckled. "More like five. Gwen gets it on purpose."

"Excuse me?"

"She hates gym, so whenever there is something she finds particularly heinous, like spiderball or field hockey, she deliberately rubs herself with poison ivy. She has the plant in her bedroom just for that purpose."

"You've been in her bedroom?" Mary Jane was surprised at how shrill her voice suddenly sounded.

"Yep. Just for a few newspaper things. She has a really great computer."

"*I'll bet she does!*" Mary Jane thought to herself. But outwardly, she simply smiled.

"Hey, Harry," Peter called.

Harry looked up from Gwen and smiled, then pulled Gwen towards them. When he got close enough he nudged Peter. "Hey, how was Le Petite Araignee? They make a killer cheeseburger, but you have to ask for it specially."

Peter glanced down at Mary Jane before answering. "Oh, yeah. We loved it. Fantastic place, Harry. I really owe you one."

"It's nothing," Harry shrugged with obvious pride. "Hey did you mention my name? I forgot to tell you to mention my name. They'd give you extra special service then."

Mary Jane and Peter couldn't help but be delighted. He seemed like the old Harry tonight.

"Our service was extra special enough. Trust me."

Harry nodded. And Mary Jane noticed Gwen's eyes had never left Peter.

"Hello, Gwen," she said flatly. And loudly.

Gwen was startled, as if surprised anyone other than Peter had been there. "Oh, Mary Jane! Hi! You look fantastic, too!"

Mary Jane frowned slightly. Did she mean Mary Jane looked fantastic, just like Peter? Or that Mary Jane looked fantastic...just like Gwen herself.

"*Have I created a monster?*" Mary Jane thought. "Thanks."

She also couldn't help but notice that Gwen's make-up was applied precisely the way Mary Jane had suggested that afternoon in the bathroom. Smart girl, that Gwen. She knew exactly what she was doing.

And she knew exactly what she wanted.

Gwen suddenly leaned towards them. "Hey, Mary Jane," she whispered in a voice loud enough to be heard by the DJ. "You have lipstick on your teeth."

Mary Jane reached up and rubbed her front tooth, her face feeling hot with an uneasy mix of embarrassment and indignity.

"There. You've got it. Most of it, anyway." Then she looked at Mary Jane's partner.

"Hey, Peter," Gwen smiled enchantingly. "I have a few article ideas for the paper. Want to drop by sometime this weekend and we can talk about it?"

"Sure," he replied.

Mary Jane looked straight ahead, not wanting to give Gwen the satisfaction of knowing she was close to tears.

"Later," Harry said as they danced off towards the refreshment table.

"Why didn't you mention that I had lipstick on my teeth?" She tried to keep her voice level.

"Huh?"

"My teeth. Lipstick. Why didn't you tell me?"

"I really didn't notice," he said, glancing around the room. "Ha! Look at Flash! He's trying to do the moon walk, and just moon walked into the speakers."

Did Peter mean he really didn't notice the lipstick on her teeth, or had Gwen just made up the whole thing to make her look ridiculous?

Either way, it wasn't good.

The DJ began to play another uptempo song, at last. And the theater kids, lead by Wendy and Bernie, ran to the center of the dance floor and began to do a clearly planned, but seemingly spontaneous routine of their own. Bill Peceau, a senior who attempted to be the school artiste — accent on the final "e" — was flaying his arms in the air. As usual he was wearing a black turtleneck. And Jennifer Campbell, a short girl with a massive chest, was dressed in a vaguely medieval gown, complete with a damsel in distress hat. She moved with regal deliberation.

And then suddenly, and inexplicably, everyone in the theater group came together in a large circle to perform a group jazz hands wave.

"Weird," mumbled Peter.

Mary Jane would have made a similar comment, but she was too busy watching Wendy, who seemed to be having a fantastic, if a bit dramatic time.

At that point, she probably was having a better time than Mary Jane.

The DJ decided it was at long last time for a break, and immediately all of the girls headed towards the bathroom. Not because of a sudden collective urge to use the facilities, but because of a collective urge to refresh makeup and hair, and, more importantly, to get the lowdown on what was happening at the dance. On breakups and couplings, on conversations overheard and after-dance plans.

Mary Jane pushed her way into the bathroom, which fortunately was the girls' locker room — with enough full length mirrors for everyone.

The first person she saw was Wendy.

"You look spectacular," she squealed, and she meant it. Wendy was in a royal blue dress that went to just above her ankle and was a perfect match for her complexion. Her hair was just as Mary Jane had done it earlier, swept into a French twist with curls bordering her face. But what made her totally off-the-charts pretty was her excitement. Her happiness seemed to radiate from within her.

"So do you, MJ! Fantastic dress! And how was dinner? Harry said he had sent you guys to someplace really amazing in the city."

She rolled her eyes, "Remind me to tell you all about it sometime."

"The Italian Villa was great, but it was really expensive. I paid around twenty-three dollars, including tip."

Mary Jane nodded in sympathy, wishing she could just tell Wendy the whole story about what had happened to them at dinner, from the price-free menus to Mrs. Stevens in the bathroom. But she did not, since she didn't want everyone to know that Peter hadn't had enough money, or that it was Mary Jane who ended up paying for their meals.

But the real reason she didn't tell Wendy everything was simply because they weren't back to normal yet.

"Twenty-three dollars," she said instead. "Whew. That is a lot."

"Yeah, but at least they had this all-you-can-eat salad bar, so we probably did get our money's worth. Especially with Bernie, who kept on going back for the..."

As Wendy spoke, Mary Jane was unable to avoid listening to a familiar voice just around the corner.

"I really like him," said the familiar voice. "But let's face it, he already has a girlfriend."

"Come on, Gwen. Don't give up so easily! He hasn't been dating Mary Jane that long. And, I mean, they've like known each other forever. I'll bet he just dates her because they've been friends for so long and he feels sorry for her."

"Do you see the way he looks at her?" Gwen asked her unseen friend.

"Do you see the way he looks at *you*? And he even yelled that you were hot!"

Mary Jane looked over to Wendy, needing desperately to go over to her and tell her all about her fears of Gwen. Never mind that they were in the middle of a cold war, Mary Jane needed her.

But Wendy had just left.

At that moment, the last remaining grains of magic went out of the dance for Mary Jane. It didn't matter that Peter had been wonderful to her all night, or that they were having an overall great time, dinner not withstanding.

A huge damper had been slammed on the evening, upon her entire life. And that damper had a name: Gwen Stacy.

* * *

Madeline Watson was asleep by the time Peter brought Mary Jane home from the dance.

By now they were both exhausted. It was well after three, and the moonlight bathed the streets in an eerie, quiet glow. Sounds were exaggerated, the odd car engine, a motorcycle roaring a few blocks away. Someone down the street turned music up loud, then quickly turned it back down again. A dog barked to be let in from the cold.

This was the one night neither Mary Jane nor Peter had a regular curfew. And although they had talked about going over to another kid's house, where the parents were hosting an all-night popcorn and slasher movie fest, they were both too tired.

Plus Mary Jane couldn't get the voice of Gwen's unseen companion out of her mind.

"Do you see the way he looks at you?"

And Gwen probably had beautifully lipstick-free teeth for the entire evening.

All Mary Jane could think of was Peter searching across the gym for a glimpse of Gwen. Peter looking over her shoulder as they danced. Peter, his eyes wandering as he talked, always hoping to see Gwen.

Even when he looked right at her, she was wondering if he wasn't wishing she was Gwen.

Then why hadn't he asked Gwen to the dance instead?

Simple, she had concluded. By the time he had fully understood the true depths of his feelings for Gwen Stacy, he had already asked Mary Jane to the dance.

"Hey, are you okay?" Peter asked as he was leaving after dropping her at home.

"Yeah. Sure. Thank you for everything, Peter."

"For what? For dragging you all over Manhattan for the supreme privilege of being abused by a bunch of pseudo-French waiters? For stepping on your toes during the last dance?"

Finally she smiled. "Thank you for all of it."

He leaned down slowly and placed a gentle kiss on her mouth. His lips were soft, and he tasted of the red punch and glazed doughnuts they served at the dance.

With one more kiss he turned to leave, then stopped. "Are you sure everything's okay?"

She nodded.

"Are you happy?"

"Absolutely."

"Good night then."

"Good night, Peter."

* * *

But everything was not okay. By morning everything was as far as possible from the blissful land of just yesterday afternoon, when everything was indeed okay.

Mary Jane felt as if she had just fallen asleep when her mother shook her awake.

"Mary Jane! Mary Jane, please wake up!"

Groggily she opened her eyes, rubbing the left one that had been pressed into her pillow. "Hi. What's going on?"

"I just got a call this morning from Mrs. Horton Stevens."

Mary Jane sat up. "Oh, Mom. That reminds me. I have to tell you something."

"Please tell me it's not true."

A terrible feeling began to unfold in the pit of Mary Jane's stomach.

Madeline continued. "She told me she gave you five hundred dollars last night. Please, please tell me it's not true."

"It's not, absolutely not!" Mary Jane cried.

"Oh, thank God," she sighed heavily.

"It was only four hundred dollars."

Madeline Watson's face drained of all color. "What?" Now her voice was a mere wisp.

"She only lent us, or me, four hundred dollars. Not five."

"Why? Why on earth did you need four hundred dollars?"

"Because we didn't realize how expensive Le Petite Araignee would be."

"Le Petite Araignee! *That's* where you had dinner last night with Peter — Le Petite Araignee? Mary Jane, that is the most expensive restaurant in New York! Why, even when we lived on Park Avenue, we only went there once or twice, and that was only when Granny Watson was paying. Le Petite Araignee? The food isn't even that good."

"I know. The Dover sole was really dry."

"Dover sole!"

"And the truffles were kind of nasty, too."

"Truffles!" Madeline pinched her temples as if in an effort to keep her head from exploding.

"Peter didn't have enough money," she said in a rush. "And so I ran into Mrs. Stevens in the ladies' room, and she offered to lend me some. Really, Mom, it was only four hundred. And I'll pay it back within a month or so, with babysitting and everything."

"But you don't understand, honey." Now her mother's voice was just tired. "Rent is due this week. And I have to pay back Mrs. Stevens the whole five hundred."

"But I only borrowed four!"

"It really doesn't matter. The truth is, I was cutting it close financially this month anyway."

Mary Jane was confused. "I thought things were so much better."

"They are. Compared to the way things used to be, we're really doing much better. Or at least we were. But the landlord wants to raise the rent. I think he really wants us to leave, so he can rent the place to his nephew."

"That's not fair!" Mary Jane was indignant.

"Doesn't matter. It's his place to rent. So if we're late with the rent this month, even by so much as a day, it will be the excuse he's been looking for to boot us out."

"Maybe we can find an even nicer place," Mary Jane said hopefully. "Really, someplace we can really love. There are a few apartments over where Wendy lives, sort of Tudor-style places. Like little English cottages. Maybe..."

"Those places are wonderful. But they are also three times the rent we pay here." Her mother shook her head. "Oh, Mary Jane, don't you understand? If we move, we'll have to go someplace else, another school district. We have a bargain here, believe it or not. We'll never find another place we can afford in this neighborhood."

"We haven't even *tried* to find a new apartment!"

"Yes, we have," her mother explained. "Ever since we moved in I've been looking for another place, a cheaper place. But they just don't exist."

Mary Jane said nothing. And finally her mother said the most awful words she could imagine. "You won't be going to Midtown, I'm afraid. Not for much longer, in any case. Good thing you're used to being the new kid at school, because it sure looks as if you'll be doing it again."

Genuine panic gripped her.

"But Mom, Mrs. Stevens doesn't need the money, like, right now. She had wads of it in her purse. It was no big deal to her. She even gave the bathroom attendant a bunch of money. Don't you see? She didn't even notice exactly how much she gave me! I'm sure if you just explain the situation, everything will be okay."

"Honey, the bottom line is that I owe a client money. That is totally unacceptable in the Skye Bleu world. It's even in the handbook. We're not allowed to accept gifts of any kind. We can't even accept tips. If she even mentions this to my boss, even whispers one single word, I'll be fired. It's as simple as that."

Mary Jane felt her throat tighten. "Mom. I'm so sorry. I had no idea that you would get into trouble."

"I know you didn't."

"Really, I can fix this! I know I can, Mom. Seriously. Somehow, I'll come up with something, and everything will be okay. It always is, isn't it? We always manage to avoid complete disaster."

Her mother said nothing. Instead she simply gave a weak shrug and left her room without even asking how the dance was. Without mentioning the gown on the floor or the shoes scattered in the corner.

This can't be happening.

For a few moments she remained in bed, watching a single beam of winter light shine through the window, dust settling along its path. Everything seemed dirty and a little soiled, as if a layer of something unpleasant had tainted the whole atmosphere.

Suddenly she jumped up, her bare feet hitting the cold

floor, and ran across the room where her purse was hanging on the back of her desk chair. She opened it up quickly, fumbling past the makeup, the combination comb and folding brush, the small mirror.

There it was. The bill from Le Petite Araignee.

There it was, a crisp slip of paper that could very well be the beginning of the end of her current happiness. It looked so innocent, a receipt like any other, computer-printed on yellow paper.

The Dover sole. The lobster. The filet mignon. The crabcakes.

Wait a minute. Crabcakes? They didn't order crabcakes.

She flipped the bill over.

Two cokes. Four glasses of water.

They charged for the water?

And two bottles of white wine.

Two bottles of white wine!

At over a hundred dollars a piece! Then came some other drinks. And after that, a few after-dinner drinks. And an after-dinner brandy. A double espresso.

It took her a moment to digest the information. And then it hit her with a glorious jolt.

This wasn't their bill after all!

There it was, something she had been longing to find. Hope.

All she had to do was go back to Le Petite Araignee, show them the incorrect bill, and the extra money would be easily refunded.

She heard her mother leaving the apartment, and smiled. Just think of how surprised, and happy, she was going to be when Mary Jane told her the good news!

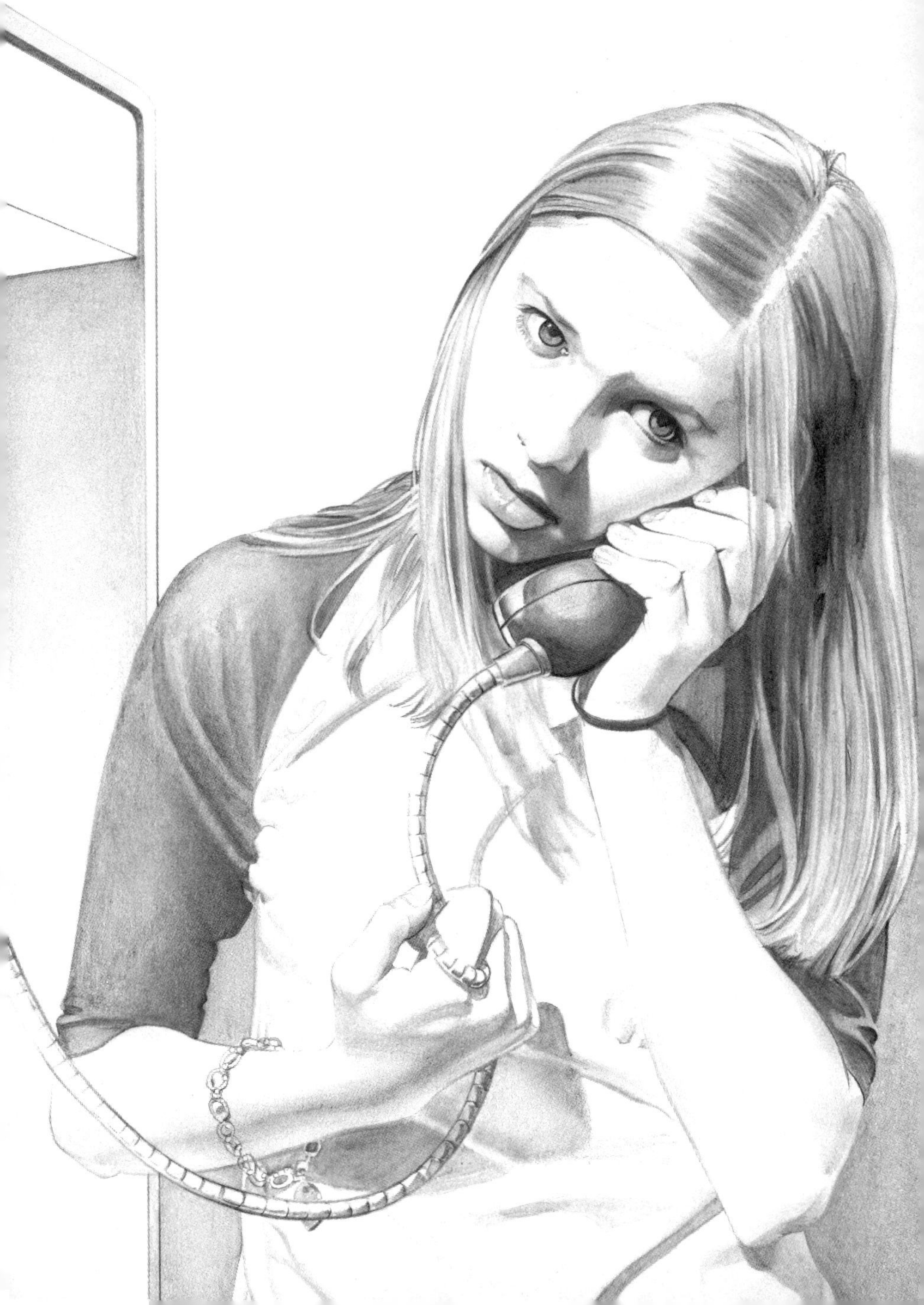

chapter 8

In the harsh reality of a glaring afternoon, with the sounds of honking horns, without the benefit of glamorous velvet darkness and twinkling lights, Le Petite Araignee had lost most of its glory.

Mary Jane stood before a very ordinary looking building. It could have been in Queens, in her own neighborhood.

Why had they been so intimidated the night before? She looked up and down the street, again nothing special. Three doors down was a copy store, and next to that was a nail salon. A bus stop was at the other end of the street, and a worn-looking bus creaked into place, belching exhaust fumes. There were cracks in the sidewalk, and the shrubbery in front of the building, which had seemed so very elegant the night before, had big brownish patches. The tiny lights that had swirled so magically now looked more like barbed wire. And there was a balled-up fast food burger wrapper, complete with extra ketchup, right under the understated — but now just small and a little dirty — Le Petite Araignee sign.

There was nothing for her to be afraid of, nothing to be embarrassed about. After all, she was in the right. They had been wrong. And she had the proof.

"I can do this," she said to herself. She pushed away the previous night's feelings of being out of place in such an elevated and rarefied atmosphere. "I'm as good as anyone," she said firmly.

Armed with a powerful attitude and the erroneous bill, Mary Jane marched right up to the front door, grabbed the big, brass knob and tried to turn it. But it was locked.

After a momentary hesitation — maybe she should just turn back — she straightened her back. It was her right– no, it was her *obligation* to set things right.

There was no doorbell, no welcoming door knocker or anything else to indicate how one could obtain admittance after hours. So she simply rapped on the thick wooden door a few times and waited. And waited. Cupping her hands over her eyes, she peered into the small, lace-covered window, and saw movement. Someone was in there. She knocked again, this time with more force.

Finally the door opened. And there stood one of the military men from the night before, only now he was stripped of his uniform. In his too-small tee shirt that read "I'm With Stupid," she couldn't remember exactly what his rank had been. But she knew for certain he had been one of their waiters.

"Yes?" His dark eyes looked her up and down. And just as obviously and swiftly, he dismissed her. "Delivery entrance is in the rear." He began to close the door.

"No, wait!" Quickly she slipped her foot between the door and the frame. "I'm not delivering anything. I ate here last night. Do you remember me?"

"I'm With Stupid" displayed no outward signs of recognition. "We have many patrons each night, Mademoiselle."

"I know. But I was with my boyfriend, a really cute..." She cleared her throat as his eyes narrowed. "I mean, he was in a tux and I was in a green gown. Not in jeans and a jacket the way I am now. And my hair was up. I was wearing pearls.

We ordered the Dover sole and..."

"That is a very popular dish."

"Yeah, well, the point is..."

"We are not open for lunch today. Come back later." He looked down pointedly at her foot, which was still blocking the door, then returned to her face. "Mademoiselle?"

"Wait a minute," she pulled out the bill. "Does this ring a bell?"

With an exasperated sigh, he glanced at the paper. "Very well. You dined here last night. I am most delighted and gratified that you enjoyed your meal. Now if you please?"

"Well see, that's just the point. The meal itself is not the issue. We were overcharged. I'm sure it was just a simple mistake. But I came here to get a refund."

His eyebrows shot up.

"Not for the whole meal. Just for the items we didn't order."

Annoyed, he looked again at the bill. "This looks correct. I see the Dover sole. The truffles."

"Ah-ha! So you do remember me, I mean us!"

"Perhaps," he shrugged lightly. "We have many customers each night." Then he looked more closely at the bill. "This is a very expensive restaurant, Mademoiselle. And you ordered our most expensive items."

"I'm aware that we ordered some expensive items. That's not the problem. Of course we paid for what we ordered, and were happy to do so. Not exactly happy. I mean, really, you guys are a little overpriced."

She could tell she was losing his interest. Quickly, she flipped over the bill. "But look here, on the back. Under 'beverages.' See? We just ordered the soda. We did not have two bottles of wine and all those drinks."

She watched his face as he studied the list, and she saw a flicker of surprise. But it passed immediately. "I am sorry, but there is nothing I can do. You paid in cash, *non?*"

"Well, yes, we did. But I don't see why that should matter."

"There is nothing to be done. *Bon jour.*" He tried to shut the door.

"May I come in for a second? It's freezing out here."

"We are closed. Please remove your foot."

Instead, she pushed her way into the hallway.

"Mademoiselle!"

"Excuse me," she called to a guy who was sliding an upholstered chair towards a table. She instantly remembered him as one of the more highly decorated members of the waiter army.

"Hello," she smiled.

He stared at her as if she had just emerged from a flying saucer.

"I'm With Stupid" scurried over to his superior officer and began speaking in rapid, hushed French. The senior waiter nodded, as if in agreement on his aid-de-camp's battle plan.

As they spoke, Mary Jane looked around the place. What a difference from the night before! The place had seemed special, amazing. Even slightly magical. But now, under the harsh overhead lights — which had been dimmed into subdued elegance during the evening — the room looked tacky.

The tables were naked. And much to her amazement, most of the tabletops were nothing more than thick plywood! Stripped of their layers of linen and glittering silver and china, they were less than ordinary. On one table was a half-eaten bagel and cream cheese, next to a paper cup of coffee.

Surely a bagel and a paper cup of coffee were not on the Le Petite Araignee menu.

The carpet was covered with crumbs, and a piece of a breadstick was off to the side.

"Young lady." The man put the chair down firmly. "Please leave at once."

"I will, as soon as you refund some of the money you guys owe me. Okay, I added it up, and it comes to two hundred and..."

"Leave at once!"

"...fifty-three dollars, forty-two cents."

"I do not recall your being here last night," he said calmly.

Mary Jane grinned. "I didn't say anything about last night. How would you know unless you saw me?"

He blinked once, then clicked his tongue and shook his head in pity. "Antoine told me you said you were here last night."

"Oh."

"For all we know, you may have found this bill outside. And now you wish to come in and extort money from Le Petite Araignee?"

"I was here last night with my boyfriend." She forced herself to remain calm. But was it possible she wouldn't get the money back? For the first time since she saw the miscalculated bill, doubt crept into her mind.

"How did you pay? You and your boyfriend. With a credit card?"

"No, with cash. A lot of cash, I might add."

"Ah, what a shame. You see, with a credit card we can see proof that it was you. And you can cancel your payment.

But with cash, well. It is simply your word against mine. And I'm afraid that the word of a young girl in jeans will not matter much to an establishment with a reputation for excellence such as Le Petite Araignee."

"Still, it seems to me that..."

"May I see it please? The bill. Perhaps it will refresh my memory."

Without waiting for her answer, he took three giant steps towards her and snatched the slip of paper from her hand. His eyes scanned the bill. Then, with a smile designed to charm any patron into selecting the most outrageously expensive and out-of-season dish, he ripped the bill in half. Then into quarters, then once again. The yellow bill fluttered to the carpet, right next to a big stain.

Mary Jane didn't miss a beat. She pulled a copy from her pocket. "I thought you might do that, so I made a bunch of copies. Most of them are at home." She scooped up the torn original. "So don't worry."

Only a momentary flash of vexation darkened his face. His voice remained soft and in control.

"You were not here last night. That I know. You are not a Le Petite Araignee customer."

And then she felt the anger rise. She was no longer frustrated or intimidated. Those feelings vanished, and all she felt was a surge of pure fury at the injustice. How dare they treat her this way, as is she was a criminal!

"So I am not a Le Petite Araignee customer?" She did everything in her power to keep from screaming. "Thank you for the compliment. And I will stay here until I get my money."

Just then the young guy who had given them free Cokes the night before came out from a back room. The moment he saw her, Mary Jane smiled and called out to him. "Hey! How are you? You remember me — I was with Peter Parker, who used to play basketball at Midtown. You saw him play with your cousin who goes to Tech and..."

"Sure, I remember..."

"Steve! Get back to the pans!" The senior guy snapped.

Steve looked at Mary Jane, then at his boss. The disarming friendliness was replaced by fear. He quickly vanished behind the door.

"Steve recognized me. He remembered us from last night. Did you see his face?" She relaxed a little. "Steve knows we were here."

"Steve is new," replied his boss. "And he does not know anything about the restaurant business yet."

"Maybe not. But it's obvious he recognized me. He even..." She was about to say that he gave them free Cokes, but stopped. She didn't want to get him into any kind of trouble.

"He even what?"

"Nothing."

"You are most welcome to bring Steve back out here, and we will ask him. However, as I said, he is new. Perhaps he is not the best person for this job after all. If his memory is so faulty, this is not a good place for him to work."

Mary Jane couldn't believe her ears. He was actually threatening to fire poor Steve simply for remembering her! She took a good look at him and realized that he would do it. He wouldn't hesitate to fire Steve just to prove his point.

So she tried a different approach. Swallowing her fury, she smiled and attempted her most pleasant cheerleader pose. "Listen, I realize this puts you all in a difficult position. But I would hate for this to get back to other guests. After all, we came here on the recommendation of one of your best customers."

That seemed to get his attention. "Yes?"

Now she was getting somewhere! A little name-dropping seemed appropriate in a place such as Le Petite Araignee. MJ took a deep breath. "Mr. Harry Osborn," she said with satisfaction.

"Who?"

"Norman Osborn's son. They had a big party here just last spring. It was written up in all the papers."

"Ah, yes. Well. Mr. Osborn's circumstances have changed dramatically. Too bad, really. But Mr. Osborn and his son are no longer considered our patrons. Now if you please, we have a great deal of work to do."

A brief stab of pity went through her for Harry. Poor guy, no longer the prize catch of the more exclusive Manhattan eating establishments and clubs.

Then Mary Jane wondered if she should mention Mrs. Horton Stevens, but realized very quickly that would be a mistake. She doubted that it would help her case at all. And she was sure Mrs. Stevens would remain a customer at Le Petite Araignee no matter what, and if she used her name now it would probably damage her mother's position as a Skye Bleu gal even further.

She was there to make things better for her mother, not worse.

The guy with the tee shirt scurried to the door and held it open, waving his arm in a grand, sweeping gesture out the door. Now she really had no choice but to leave.

"This is so messed up," she said. The guy with the tee shirt had the grace to look slightly embarrassed. Just slightly. She began to head toward the door when she paused and looked at the "I'm With Stupid" shirt.

"Do you work with him a lot?" she asked, pointing her thumb at the senior waiter. The door holder seemed uncertain how to react. So he simply shrugged and, evidently deciding it couldn't hurt to admit this one thing, nodded once.

"That's what I thought." She walked out of the restaurant, then over her shoulder retorted, "Now your shirt makes complete sense."

The door slammed.

And in an instant her one flash of satisfaction was gone. Along, it seemed, with the money.

Perhaps she should have approached things differently. Maybe she should have come with her mother. But that probably wouldn't have made any difference. It might have been even more terrible, and the result would have been the same, only her mother would have been there to share in the shame.

Then again, she could have asked Peter to come along.

But even the thought of that made her cringe. The only thing that would have accomplished is to completely humiliate him. After all, it was Peter who had asked her to the restaurant in the first place. With his slightly old-fashioned ideas, even older than his vintage tux, he was convinced he should have paid. The only reason he let her pick up the check was that he had no idea how expensive it was, and she absolutely insisted.

Had he known, well. He would have done anything in his power to help. Yet there was nothing he could have done. And how hideous it would have been for him to face the sneering staff in broad daylight! No, she was glad Peter hadn't been there, and was even more relieved that he had absolutely no idea what was happening.

And she intended to keep it that way. This was her problem, hers alone, and she would solve it.

She couldn't dwell any longer on what had just transpired, on how she should or shouldn't have handled the situation. What else she could have done, or snappy comebacks she could have made to the staff. Now there was only one thing Mary Jane needed to think about, and that was how to get the money back to her mother. As soon as possible.

Otherwise, by spring she'd be the new kid in some other high school.

Again.

* * *

Mary Jane spent the rest of the day looking for a job. She couldn't depend on babysitting to get enough money to pay her mother back. Besides, she'd already turned down a ton of sitting jobs, mainly because of the play, but also because of Peter.

She had to do something. Anything.

On her way home she stopped at almost every store she passed, from card and gift shops to restaurants and even an auto repair store. The only place she skipped was the butcher shop, and that was simply because the owner, an otherwise friendly guy, always creeped her out with his blood-splattered apron.

But all of the shops had already hired their extra holiday workers.

By late afternoon she was desperate and willing to do almost anything for the money. And that anything turned out to be at Queens Plaza shopping mall. Mary Jane Watson was to do promotional modeling at Grimby's Department Store. It sounded glamorous, until she discovered what "promotional modeling" meant: strolling through the ground floor of Grimby's spraying perfume on unwitting passersby. In other words, she was to be a spritzer girl.

The man who hired her, Mr. Tiller, took an appraising look at her jeans and pink sweater.

"Do you have something else to wear? We're hoping for a more sophisticated look." He himself was wearing an impossibly well-tailored suit, and MJ noticed his nails were actually buffed.

"Well," Mary Jane said, smoothing her hair. "I do have a long green gown. It's a bit formal."

"Green?" He brightened. "And formal? Why, that would be perfect for the holiday season. Festive, you know."

Mr. Tiller looked at her over his clipboard. "Let me see, I do have two other girls to see before I make a decision."

"I wore it last night to Le Petite Araignee," she added, attempting to look as worldly as possible.

"Fantastic!" He grinned broadly, exposing a full set of tiny teeth. They were like baby teeth, small and square and plentiful. She was so busy staring at his teeth that she almost missed the fact that she was hired. On the spot.

For the not-so-sophisticated salary of eight dollars an hour, Mary Jane would be the new Passion's Flame girl.

Mr. Tiller tapped a pen against a tiny tooth. "Or maybe you should be a Sporty Chick."

"Excuse me?"

"You know, Sporty Chick. The new perfume with the girl doing cartwheels. It's in all the magazines."

"Yes, of course," she agreed, although she really wasn't quite sure what he meant. "I can do cartwheels, if you need me to."

He looked shocked. "Cartwheels? No. Not in a formal gown."

"I see what you mean," she crossed her arms. "And I guess the aisles would get too crowded. With all the shoppers..."

She realized she was babbling. She also realized he was beginning to doubt his wisdom in choosing her. "Um, when should I start?"

He stared at her for a few moments, then shrugged. "The store's open until ten this evening for holiday shopping." He consulted his watch. "Can you be here at six?"

"Tonight?" But she had a date with Peter!

"Is that a problem?"

"No, not at all, Mr. Tiller." It's only a problem if I want to have a boyfriend. Or a life.

"Very well. I'll see you in a couple of hours."

"Great. Thank you," she shook his hand and, with a false smile, left the mall.

Great, she thought to herself. Just great.

* * *

The first thing Mary Jane noticed when she entered the apartment was the smell of cigarette smoke.

"Mom?" She threw down her purse.

"Yes?" Her mother stepped out of the kitchen, waving her hand in front of her face. "Hi, honey."

"Have you been smoking?"

"No," she said quickly. Then her shoulders sagged. "Well, maybe a little."

"But you quit months ago!"

"I know. It's just that, well, I was feeling a little nervous. And I thought a cigarette or two might make me feel better."

"Did it?"

"No. But it did give me something to do." Madeline Watson brushed by MJ and went over to the coffee table in the living room, where she immediately began to straighten out magazines that were already perfectly straight. "I didn't really start smoking again."

"Well, that's good." Mary Jane watched as her mother picked up a dust rag that had been on the television and began to wipe away invisible smudges from the side tables and the back of the couch. "Are you okay, Mom?"

"Yes. Well." She bent closer to scrub a particularly stubborn invisible smudge. "I heard from Mrs. Stevens today. And she booked an appointment for tomorrow through the Skye Bleu regional manager."

"Miss Bates?"

"Yep, Miss Bates. So I have to give her the money she lent you by then. She says it was five hundred dollars."

"No! It was only four hundred!"

Her mother stopped and stared at her.

"I didn't mean 'only,'" she amended. "I just mean…"

"It's okay, Mary Jane. It really doesn't matter whether it's four hundred or four million."

"I got a job though!"

"You what?" Madeline balled up the dust rag.

"I got at job at Queens Plaza. So I'll be able to start paying you back."

"Really?" A glimmer of hope brightened her mother's features. "Oh, honey, that's wonderful! How much will you be making?"

"Eight dollars an hour. But I'll work as much as I possibly can. I'm even starting tonight."

The hope faded from her face. "Eight dollars. That's really wonderful." But her voice was defeated.

"We'll get through this, Mom. I promise."

Her mother smiled sadly. "Of course we will."

"Hey, do you have a date tonight with your new boyfriend?"

She was busy folding the dust rag into a careful square. "No. No, he has to work. Maybe next week sometime."

Mary Jane felt an ache in her throat, knowing how very worried her mother was, but also knowing there was nothing she could do to help. At least not right now, at that very moment.

"Peter called," her mother said.

"Oh, thanks."

Then her mother went back into the kitchen, and MJ heard the sound of a match strike. Within a few moments she could smell the cigarette smoke.

She went over to the phone, thinking of excuses she could use with Peter. It wouldn't be easy to get out of their date. But she had to work.

Just then the phone rang. It was Peter.

"Hi," she began. "I was just about to call you!"

"Really?" He sounded a little weird.

"Yeah. What's up?" Maybe she could say she was sick, not feeling well — which was absolutely true. Or that she had a big paper due Monday she had forgotten about. Or...

"Hey, I'm really sorry, but I can't make it tonight," he said.

"Excuse me?" Mary Jane stiffened.

"Yeah, I'm really sorry. Something came up."

"What came up?" Even though he had merely beaten her to the punch, she couldn't keep the hurt tone from her voice.

He was cancelling on *her*!

"Well, I was thinking of telling you I wasn't feeling all that great," he began. "Then I was going to tell you a bogus story about a mysterious paper I suddenly remembered is due on Monday."

"Were you?"

"Yep. But in the end I've just decided to go with the truth."

She turned her back on a puff of cigarette smoke that wafted from the kitchen.

"What's the truth?"

"Well, you see. Gwen Stacy thinks we should try to get a Spider-Man story for the paper."

"Gwen?"

"So we're going to prowl the city in search of either Spider-Man, or people who have seen him. Isn't that a great idea?"

"Terrific. Wish I'd thought of it."

"Are you okay with this? I mean, if you want to, you can come along. But it might not be that much fun for you."

She took a deep breath and almost told him about her job. But at the last moment decided not to. She was too upset about everything, from her encounter at Le Petite Araignee to her mother smoking again. And now this.

No. She wouldn't tell him about her job and that she couldn't have seen him tonight anyway. "Okay. Well, have a good time with Gwen."

"Wait a minute! Don't be that way, MJ! It's not like that, it's..."

But she didn't hear what he was going to say, because she had done something she hardly ever did, and had never done to Peter: She hung up on him.

The moment she did, she regretted it. It was too late.

She waited a few seconds, then a few minutes, hoping he'd call back. But he didn't. And she was just about to call him back when she suddenly realized she didn't know what she'd say.

That she was jealous of Gwen Stacy? That because of his restaurant choice of the night before, she had to work?

That very soon, MJ and her mother may have to move?

No, there was really nothing she could say to explain herself. To explain how very hurt she was, how terribly upset.

And how she needed him now more than ever.

Instead she stared at the silent telephone. Then she changed into the green gown she had worn with such hopeful joy less than twenty-four hours before. And she went to her new job.

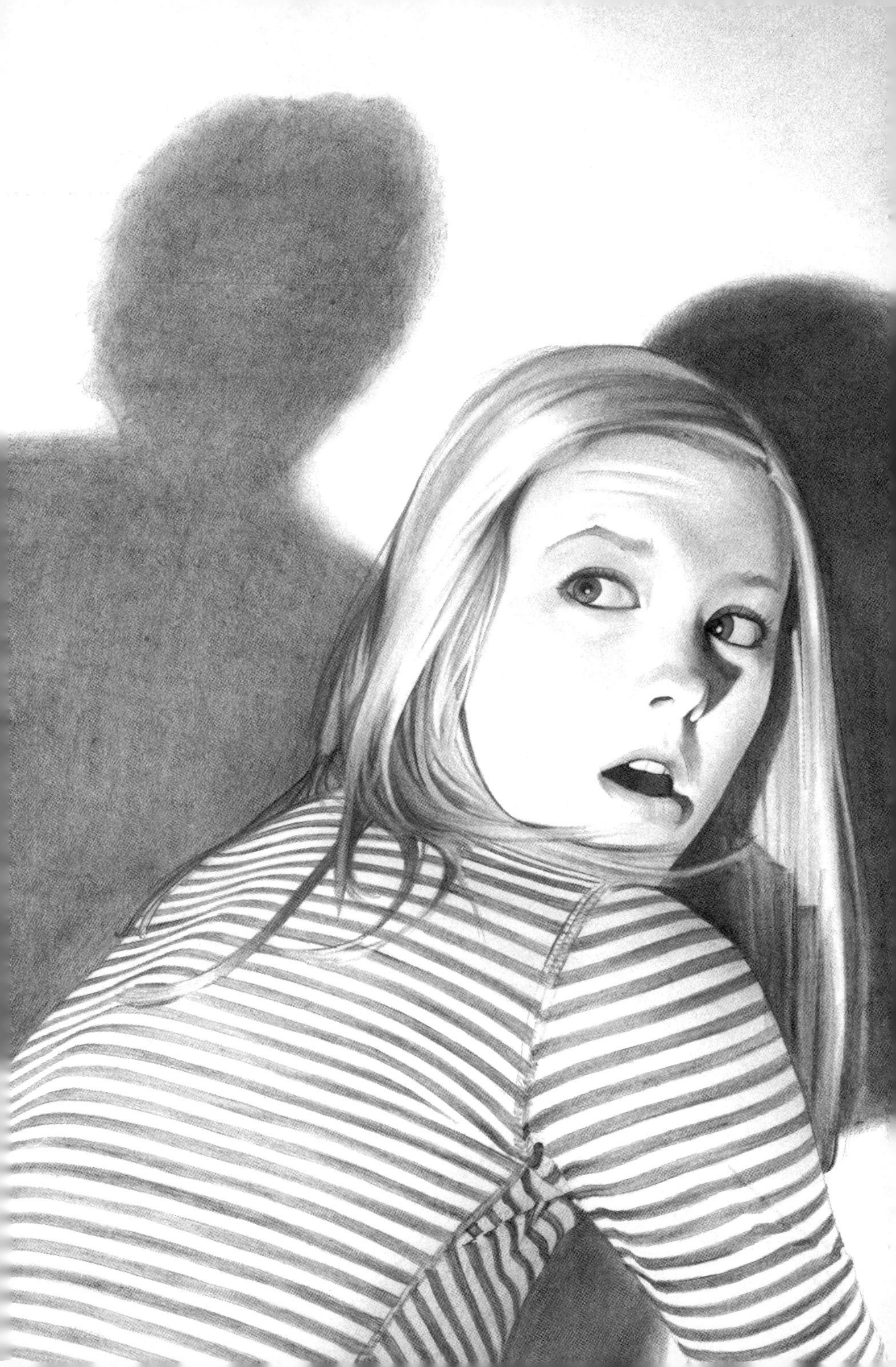

chapter 9

By the middle of the following week, Mary Jane was certain of several things.

One, she heartily detested her job. It had made the jump from mildly annoying to actively hateful sometime during Sunday's ten-hour marathon stretch. In fact, she had even toyed with the notion of stopping by the butcher shop to see if they needed help. Just about anything had to be better than being a Grimby's spritzer girl.

It was astonishing how many dirty looks, verbal abuses and occasional physical threats a person could receive in a single afternoon simply by strolling about in a formal gown, randomly spraying an obnoxious scent, and chanting "Passion's Flame by Ricardo. Inflame your passion. Passion's Flame by Ricardo. Inflame your passion."

She also knew she had developed an active dislike for Passion's Flame by Ricardo. By Wednesday it was impossible to get away from the smell. The "sensuous embrace of gardenia, rose, neroli, and amber designed to stir the senses" (or so the copy read) so far had only stirred up a massive headache. Even after she showered and washed her hair, the smell lingered, as if it had embedded itself under her skin. And it wasn't her imagination. When she would be chatting with people in the hallways at school, or even outside, they would stop mid-sentence and sniff.

"Do you smell something?" they would say, "they" being everyone from Wendy to Harry to Bernie to her physics teacher and Ms. Krumplesteater, the volleyball coach slash musical choreographer.

"No, what?" She would always reply innocently, sniffing once or twice herself just for good measure.

"I don't know," they would frown, clearly disturbed. So far the scent had reminded them of disinfectant, Harry's great Aunt Ida, discount air freshener, and her personal favorite, rancid nail polish remover. Not a single person had mentioned a sensuous embrace of any kind. And a kid in the library known to be a complete hypochondriac had even wondered aloud if the strange, mysterious scent indicated the onset of a brain tumor.

As a direct side effect of her utter loathing of the part-time job, MJ had also started to hate the formal gown she had so recently adored. Especially the shoes. What had been so wonderfully dainty and delicate on her feet the night of the dance had morphed into evil size seven-and-a-half twin torture chambers. Even the sight of them made her shudder. And since she was working every day, the small blisters had happily grown into honking deformities. At least she was used to foot pain from all the years of ballet.

And speaking of ballet, the job also made her a chronic no-show at the Manhattan School of Ballet. She'd only been able to make it to one lesson in the past ten days. Now that she was kept from attending classes, she really missed them. One thing, at least, became clear: Maybe ballet wasn't going to be her entire life, but that didn't make her love it any less.

All this for only eight dollars an hour, minus taxes. So in reality she was earning about five dollars and forty cents.

"Don't worry," smiled Mr. Tiller with his full set of baby teeth. "You'll get most of that back in your tax return."

"When will that be?" She'd asked eagerly, rubbing her foot.

"Sometime after April 15th," he'd stated cheerfully.

"Great." She tried to be equally cheerful, but couldn't help wonder where they might be living by spring.

She also knew that Peter scored a major coup the night he canceled their date. Not that she found out directly from Peter himself. Instead she found out the way everyone else did: by seeing it in the paper.

There on the front page of the *Daily Bugle* was a full-color photograph of Spider-Man in action. And beneath it, in tiny type, "Photo by Peter Parker."

As Mary Jane looked at the picture, she felt two different emotions battling for control in her chest. She was excited for Peter, but couldn't help feeling a little disappointed. Shut out. Just as Gwen Stacy had predicted, they managed to find Spider-Man in action. They weren't together, which was the only aspect of the tale that brought a smile to MJ's lips. In fact, Peter had snapped pictures of Spider-Man right after Gwen had interviewed him. Which was just before he nabbed two would-be bank robbers as they drove away on Queens Boulevard. Spider-Man had done some sort of *Three Stooges*-type of move, bumping their heads together as he held them by the scruffs of their necks.

So Peter's big break was also Gwen's. This was something they would always share. This was something the two of them had done together. This was something that made Mary Jane want to puke.

"The Spider-Man: Good or Evil" blared the *Bugle*. The picture they used was not one of Peter's best. The Spider-Man was a little out of focus, as if jumping back from the camera. Still, it was unmistakably the real deal, the insect guy himself.

Now Peter was a real photographer, a professional. His dream had come true, which was great. But he hadn't even called Mary Jane to tell her the news. Not so great. Those photo-snapping fingers probably worked just fine when it came to dialing Gwen Stacy's number.

As if all of that wasn't enough, her job combined with her missing-in-action boyfriend, there was yet another element to make this particular Wednesday especially bright. They wanted her at Grimby's by four o'clock that afternoon, meaning she would miss play rehearsal. Again. And she'd already had to skip out early for the past two practices.

Both Mr. Toby and Ms. Krumplesteater were not pleased, to say the least.

"This is a serious matter, Miss Watson." Mr. Toby pointed his long finger at her. "You cannot commit to being in a musical, and then not show up at rehearsals."

"I know. But this is sort of an emergency," she explained.

"I understand," Ms. Krumplesteater said in a tone that clearly indicated she did not understand at all. "But really, Mary Jane, this is terrible timing. We're uniting the whole cast for a major scene today. And you're by far the best dancer we've got."

Mary Jane felt a sudden rush of pleasure. "Really?"

"Yes, really. You're the backbone of the chorus."

"Thank you. I appreciate that. But really, it is something of an emergency." As in, if I don't work, we'll be booted out of the house. As in, if I don't work, I'll be going to Random High next semester.

"Very well," Mr. Toby said in a stern voice, as stern as he could possibly be wearing Eliza Doolittle's cape for a scene he was blocking. "Just try not to miss any more rehearsals."

"I'll try." She felt like a total liar. She knew for a fact that Grimby's wanted her to spritz early all the following week.

And as it was, Wendy was clearly ticked off at her.

"You're missing rehearsal again?" Wendy said, her mouth wide open in accusatory disbelief.

"Yeah, but hopefully I can make it the rest of the week."

"Hopefully?" This time it was said as a semi-scoff.

"No, really. I have to be someplace else." Of course that was true. But ironically enough, she would have much rather been at play practice. After all, walking up to complete strangers wearing uncomfortable shoes and assaulting them in some drive-by perfume spritzing was no picnic. Compared to that, walking around in synchronized circles to a recording of My Fair Lady in sneakers was an absolute pleasure.

"Yeah, right," Wendy said. "You just want to miss today's practice because it's the first with me in it, with the principles in the Covent Garden scene."

Then Wendy walked away. It didn't really make much sense to her, but then, nothing seemed to make much sense to MJ since the dance.

Nothing at all.

* * *

He called her name just as she was about to turn the corner after school.

"Mary Jane! Hey, Mary Jane!'

She stopped and bit her lower lip. All she'd wanted to do since Saturday was talk to him. But now that he was right there, all she wanted to do was run away.

Instead she turned around and smiled. "Hey, Tiger." She even managed a convincing semi-wave.

Peter grinned and jogged towards her. "Hey! I've been looking all over for you."

"Have you?"

When he reached her he stopped. She noticed he wasn't even out of breath, although he'd just run at least three blocks. "Yeah. Don't you have rehearsal?"

She didn't want him to know about her job, because that would lead straight to the reason she had to take the stupid job in the first place. Which would in turn head directly into having to pay back Mrs. Stevens, her mother, losing the apartment, and the humiliation she would always feel at the mention of the words "Le Petite Araignee" and "Dover sole."

She didn't want him to know anything. Yet at the same time, she longed to tell him everything. This was, after all, her friend Peter.

What she really wanted to say was, "Why haven't you called me? Do you like Gwen better than me? Are you dumping me in slow, photographic stages?"

"I have to be someplace else," she said lamely. And of course she knew exactly, predictably, naturally what his next question would be.

"Where do you have to be?"

"Just someplace."

"Ballet?"

"No."

"Not ballet?"

"No, not ballet." He looked perplexed, and she suddenly felt angry, angry because he liked Gwen. Angry because he hadn't called her all week. Angry because she had a strong feeling that he was about to break up with her, to make it official.

"Oh, I was just wondering," he began.

"What is this, the Spanish Inquisition?" MJ snapped.

Peter jumped as if he'd been touched with a live wire. "Sorry," he said softly. "I was just wondering if I could walk you to wherever you're going."

"No, you can't." Then she looked at him closely, at the face she knew so well, yet wanted to know even better. At the blue eyes that were so familiar, but somehow so distant. "I'm sorry," she sighed. "I'm just a little tired."

"I know what you mean," he said casually.

"Oh, hey, great job on the photo!"

Then he brightened. "Really? Thanks! Which one did you like better, the one on the *Midtown Gazette*, or the one in the *Bugle?*"

She hadn't even seen the school paper yet. She'd deliberately avoided it — it was too closely linked to all things Gwen.

"I see why the *Bugle* picked the one they did," she hedged. Peter nodded, and she continued. "I mean, it was more matter-of-fact. But I liked the Midtown one more. It was artistic." That was bound to be a good guess.

"I liked that one too." He smiled.

149

"Have you gotten any more assignments from the *Bugle?*"

"Nah. The editor in chief pretty much said if I happen to come upon a crime scene, and happen to have my camera, and happen to have film in the camera, and he happened to have the time, then he'd be perfectly happy to look at what I shoot. He was really cranky, this old guy named Jameson. I'll take Gwen as an editor over him any day."

"Oh."

"So no real assignments. Guess I'll be with the *Midtown Gazette* a while longer. Or until I graduate. Whichever comes first."

I doubt Gwen will be letting you out of her clutches anytime soon.

"I tried to call you a few times," he said. "The phone was busy. I figured you were online or something. So I tried to instant message you, but got no response."

"Maybe my mom was using the computer," she shrugged, wondering whether or not to believe him.

"Maybe," he sounded as if he didn't quite believe her either. "Um, Mary Jane?"

"Yes?"

"Did you have a good time at the dance? With me?"

The dance. The dinner. The disaster.

She winced involuntarily, then tried to smile. "Sure I did!" Even she could hear the fake, wavering quality in her voice. But what could she do?

For a long moment he said nothing. Then he smiled sadly. "Okay, Mary Jane. I get it."

"No, really!" But if she explained any further, she would have to tell him the whole story. And she could never do that. It would hurt him too much.

"I said it's okay." He reached out and touched her shoulder. Even through her jacket and sweater she could feel the warmth of his hand. "I have some film to develop. Take care, Mary Jane. If you ever need me, you know where to find me. And I'll always be here for you."

She swallowed, her eyes stinging with tears. "Peter, I..."

But he just squeezed her shoulder once. And then he turned around and jogged back to school, back to the *Gazette* office. Back to Gwen Stacy.

She stood for a while and watched him as his figure grew smaller, his impossibly graceful gait. He jumped over three bicycles piled by the flagpole without missing a step.

And as he disappeared, she put her hand on her left shoulder, where he had touched her last. It was still warm.

* * *

By the time she got back to her apartment to change into the green formal gown and the dreaded shoes, her mother was pacing in the living room. Even the open window couldn't disguise the smell of cigarette smoke.

"Mary Jane," she said without even a hello. "Did you give Mrs. Stevens one of the new lipsticks?"

"Huh? Can I put my books down first?"

"Miss Norma Bates from Skye Bleu just called, and she is absolutely livid. Mrs. Horton Stevens wants one of the lipsticks from the New Horizon line."

"Miss Bates' first name is Norma? So she's Norma Bates?" She was unable to repress a giggle. "That explains why she's so psycho."

"Mary Jane, this isn't funny."

"Sorry."

"The New Horizon line isn't supposed to be available until after January." Her mother was genuinely upset, and suddenly Mary Jane felt terrible.

Couldn't she do *anything* right?

"Mom, I didn't mean to get you into trouble. It's just that Mrs. Stevens saw me in the ladies' room of Le Petite Araignee and noticed the lipstick."

"Was it Fleur de Mauve?"

"Yes, I think so. I'm sorry."

"Mary Jane, that particular shade was supposed to be the cornerstone of Skye Bleu's spring collection."

"Okay," she answered, still not sure why this was such a big deal.

"And when Mrs. Stevens couldn't get it from Skye Bleu, she took the lipstick over to every department store cosmetics counter in town to find a match. And now every cosmetics company has a sample, drawn on her own excellent-quality stationery by Mrs. Stevens herself, of the new secret shade coming from the New Horizon line. The secret's out. And already, in just two days, Lady Baccara and Cosmetique have managed to replicate the shade."

Mary Jane was beginning to understand why this was such a big deal.

"Oh, no."

"Oh, yes."

"Mom, I..."

"They fired me, Mary Jane. I no longer have a job."

Mary Jane was speechless.

"My new friend," her mother started, then cleared her

throat. "My boyfriend has offered to help us out for a month or so, but after that. Well. I don't know what I'm going to do. What we're going to do."

"This is all my fault."

"No, it isn't, honey. Not really. I never should have given you the sample lipstick to begin with."

But Mary Jane didn't hear. All she knew was that from one dinner, from one lousy meal, things had spiraled out of control.

"I'm so sorry," was all she could say.

"It will be okay," her mother's voice sounded like a distant echo. She really didn't hear individual words, just an overall soothing tone, like the way you'd speak to a hurt animal. Her mother kept on talking, something about dinner in a few days with the new boyfriend. And would Mary Jane be able to come? He's bringing his kid too. It's about time everyone met. After all, he has been kind enough to help them over this rough spot and...

"Yeah, sure. I can't wait. Um, I have to get to work now."

Her mother continued speaking, but in a numb fog Mary Jane no longer listened. She simply slipped on the green dress, shoved her feet into the painful shoes, and left for work.

After all, someone in the Watson household had to work.

* * *

For once, she was actually glad to be at work. All that spritzing kept her mind off everything else.

At one point she saw Harry and Gwen Stacy enter Grimby's side door, next to Men's Suits and Outer Wear, and she spritzed in the other direction until they were gone.

The store was getting more and more crowded the closer they got to Christmas. Mr. Tiller predicted a banner year for Grimby's Department Store, and Mary Jane was glad that at least someone was having a banner year.

And then something lovely happened: She got her first paycheck! It wasn't enough to pay the rent, just over one hundred dollars, but still it was fantastic. Before she left for the evening she cashed it in the payroll department, since her mom needed the cash. They couldn't wait the extra few days it would take for the check to clear.

She was almost happy as she packed up for home, but slightly annoyed with herself for forgetting to bring more comfortable shoes for the trip back. She had a sudden urge to buy a new pair with her employee discount, and stopped herself.

"Talk about defeating the whole purpose," she laughed. No, she would take the cash straight home and give it to her mom.

The lights were being switched off all over the mall, and security guards held the doors open for the departing employees. She left with a very exhausted Santa, who offered her a ride in his little sports car. Although she'd seen him around, she didn't know him very well.

"Thanks, Santa," she said shaking his hand. "I'll pass on the ride. But can you work on everything else on my list?"

"Sure," he winked. "As long as you've been nice."

"There's always a catch," she said over her shoulder as she walked to the main street. She could hear him laughing as he started the engine.

What would she ask for if she had the chance? If there was really a Santa, she would ask for a good job for her mother.

A really good job, one she loved, one that made her excited to face the world each day.

Next, she'd want things to be straightened out with Wendy. She missed her, especially now, with everything else that was going on.

And Peter. She would want everything to be the way it was before the dance, before Gwen Stacy. Before her own doubts. Maybe she could even wish for Uncle Ben to still be alive, for...

And then she noticed someone was following her.

Was it Santa?

Nope. She saw his car speed out of the parking lot.

The fine hairs on the back of her neck prickled. It was after ten o'clock on a Wednesday night. The streets were empty. Except for Mary Jane. And someone just a few steps behind her.

She walked a little faster, and so did the person behind her. Her feet were hurting, but she picked up the pace.

And so did the other person.

Maybe they were just in a hurry to get to where they were going. Maybe they were meeting friends in a restaurant, or were late for an important meeting. Maybe they just had to go to the bathroom.

An arm reached out and grabbed her.

"No!" She kicked back with her heel and elbowed him in the stomach. He grunted, and she turned to see him.

He was a tall man wearing a black ski mask. That's all her mind could take in. That, and the fact that she could not afford to have him take her purse. Not with all that money.

"Hand it over," he grunted, struggling as he pulled her back towards him.

How could he be so strong?

"No!" she shouted, and hit him in the nose. He staggered back and swore, and she started to run. But with her long dress and heels, she didn't get very far before he caught up to her.

And suddenly Mary Jane realized that the money wasn't worth it.

"Here," she shoved her purse at him. "Take it."

And then, in what seemed like an impossible flash, a red and blue creature swooped down from a nearby building and slammed into the mugger.

"Oh, no. It's you!" The mugger squealed from where he lay on the pavement, his low, threatening voice now high-pitched and frightened. "Hey, Spidey. You know I'm just playing, right?"

The Spider-Man turned to Mary Jane. "Are you okay?" His voice was muffled behind the mask.

"Yeah, I'm...Hey! He's getting away!" The guy in the ski mask was limping as fast as he could down the street.

With almost casual ease, Spider-Man shot webs from his wrists, which grabbed the escaping mugger. A slight tug and he was flung back like he was on a gigantic rubber band.

"Are you all right?" Spider-Man asked Mary Jane as he reeled the mugger in. He looked around for a moment, then suspended him from a lamp post in a big web sack.

"Yes." She bent down to pick up her purse, but he reached it first. "Thank you," she said as he handed it over.

"You're welcome."

They stood there for a moment, just looking at each other. Then he spoke in a voice that was at once strange, yet somehow familiar. "What are you doing out at this hour, and all dressed up?" He cleared his throat. "A date?"

The tied-up guy grunted again. "Bro, can you loosen these a little?"

Spider-Man waved his hand to silence him, and another shot of sticky web flew out. The mugger groaned.

"Were you on a date?" Spider-Man repeated to Mary Jane. There was a tightness to his tone. But between the mask and the darkness, it was difficult to see details. Although from what she could tell, he was as well-built as she remembered from their last encounter.

"Not a date. A job."

"A job?" He seemed surprised. Then he deepened his voice. "A job. I see. Well, Miss, you should be more careful."

"Thank you, I will be."

"What kind of job?"

"Excuse me?"

"What kind of job do you have? All dressed up on a school night. I mean, so late at night."

Did his voice crack?

"Hey, these things really hurt!" The mugger wailed. Both Spider-Man and Mary Jane ignored him.

"I'm a perfume spritzer at Grimby's Department Store."

"Over at Queens Plaza?"

"Yes. You're sure familiar with Queens, aren't you?"

"I make it my business to be familiar with neighborhoods."

Just then the wind shifted, and she got a whiff of something, a scent she recognized.

She could have sworn she smelled photo developing chemicals. Sometimes she could smell them on Peter. On days like today. When he was developing film.

"Hey, wait a minute," she said. She stepped closer to him and reached out her hand to touch his shoulder. It was muscular, hard.

"The bus is coming," he put his own hand on her shoulder and guided her to the corner. "Do you have a fare card?"

"I have a fare card," the mugger offered. "If you let me go, she can have mine. Deal?"

"No deal," Spider-Man said over his shoulder. "So do you have a fare card, Mar—Miss?"

He almost said her name! But how could he know?

"Yes, but..." The bus was pulling up. And then she whispered, "Peter, is that you?"

"Ah, make a move already," the mugger heckled. With that Spider-Man aimed his wrist and shot a string of web over his mouth. "Grambal fwaght," was his final garbled exclamation.

Mary Jane smiled, and Spider-Man's voice seemed to smile behind his mask as well. "Take care, Miss. And be more careful."

With that he was gone, collecting the mugger with one easy swipe. But as she sat on the bus, she touched her shoulder.

And it was still warm from his hand.

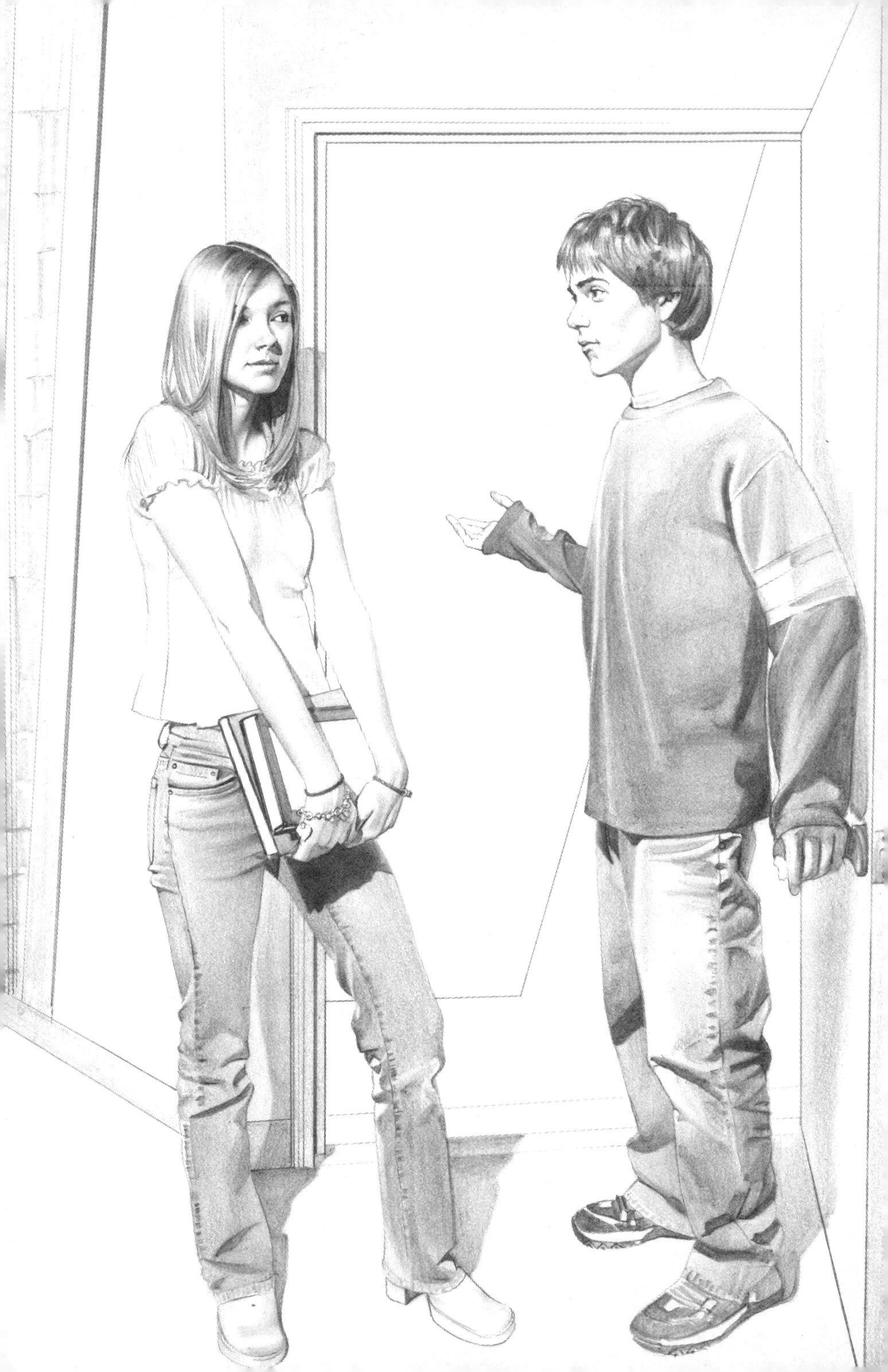

chapter 10

It was ridiculous, really, the mere thought that Peter Parker could be Spider-Man. Truly absurd.

After her initial freak-out at the whole thing, all she could concentrate on were the details of Spider-Man, of how he spoke. Of what he said.

No way could he have been Peter!

Still, there was something about him. And what about the scent of film developing chemicals, the slightly-sour, acrid smell?

That was all she could think about on the bus ride home. Not that she had almost been mugged — or worse. Not that she had some money to finally give to her mom.

And it became even more absurd when she told her mother what had happened. Her mom made her call the police to report the would-be crime.

"But nothing really happened, Mom," Mary Jane protested.

Still, her mother dialed the local precinct herself and stood by as she gave the desk clerk all the details, what few there were. But what was really interesting was how she seemed to question her more about Spider-Man than about the would-be mugger. Every time she would begin to describe a detail, such as "tall" and "wore a black knit ski mask," the woman on the other end taking down the information would invariably ask, "Do you mean Spider-Man?"

When the semi-report was over, Mary Jane finally gave the hard-earned, and even harder-kept cash to her mother, who was indeed pleased.

"Oh, Mary Jane! Thank you!" She clutched the money to herself the way Mary Jane used to hug her teddy bear for security and comfort. Madeline had withdrawn five hundred dollars from their account a few days earlier to pay back Mrs. Stevens, even though Mary Jane again protested that she had only borrowed four hundred.

Which left Mary Jane shaking her head in wonderment. Why was she unable to convince *anyone* of *anything* these days?

And then she had a sudden urge. As her mother was brushing her teeth in the bathroom, Mary Jane picked up the phone, and after only a moment's hesitation — it was, after all, after eleven o'clock — she called Peter.

"Hello," he answered. Not tired, or groggy. Clearly he'd been awake.

"Hi, Peter, it's..."

"Oh, hi, MJ. What's up?"

She paused. He sounded innocent enough, as if he'd been at home all evening. Maybe this was a crazy thought, but she had to follow her instincts.

"I just thought I'd call." She cleared her throat. "What did you do tonight?"

"Nothing much. I stayed late at school developing pictures, which was a total waste of time. They all suck. Most were too grainy to be of any use, although there is a great picture of my thumb over the lens. That one turned out beautifully. Then I helped Aunt May with her fruitcakes. Do you think anyone ever eats them? My theory is that the same five cakes get passed around, year after year. I swear Aunt May is the only person on the planet making them. And have you ever seen that fruit they use in those cakes? Creepy. There are these fluorescent green cherries that..."

Whoa, she thought. Someone should switch to decaf.

She'd had just about enough.

"I was mugged tonight," she stated flatly.

She heard him suck in his breath. "Oh, no! Mary Jane, are you okay? What happened?" He sounded genuinely upset, and surprised.

"I'm fine. Spider-Man came to my rescue."

"Really? That's fantastic! What was he like? Did you get a chance to speak to him? What does he look like up-close? How did he stop the guy? Did he do any of his awesome moves? Did you know how strong he is? He can lift..."

Mary Jane held the receiver at arm's length and rolled her eyes. He sounded like a little kid talking about his favorite cartoon character. His voice was rising to such a high pitch, she was certain neighborhood dogs would start to howl.

"I just thought you might want to know," she said wearily.

"This is so cool! Hey, mind if I interview you for the school paper?"

"Sure, although there's not much to tell."

"Are you kidding? Mary Jane — you were rescued by Spider-Man! That is so incredibly cool!"

"Yeah, well. Listen, I'm really exhausted now. I'm going to bed."

"Oh, sure. You'd better get lots of sleep. I mean, if I had just been rescued by Spider-Man, I wouldn't be able to sleep for about a week. I've seen him, of course. How else could I have photographed him? But to have seen him in action. Wow! I hear he's like a big blur...."

"Peter? Good night."

"...and that all you see is....Oh, okay. Sleep well, MJ. I'll see you tomorrow."

"Good night," she yawned.

"Good night," he said giddily.

Two things are certain, she thought to herself as she finally slipped into bed. One, whatever had happened, she had made Peter Parker's day.

And two, there was absolutely no way in a million years he could be Spider-Man.

"What was I thinking?" She murmured as she scrunched a wonderfully soft pillow under her head. Within moments, she was asleep.

About a half mile away, Peter Parker was wide-awake. Still fully dressed, he flopped onto his bed, his fingers linked under his head, and stared up at the ceiling. And as he thought about that evening's events, a slow, satisfied smile spread across his face.

* * *

Perhaps the very last person on the planet, male or female, Mary Jane wanted to see lounging against her locker first thing in the morning was Gwen Stacy. So naturally, that was the precise vision that awaited her the next day right before first period.

"Mary Jane!" Gwen called.

And what made the whole thing so much more vexing was that she was looking incredible that morning, in tight black jeans and an even tighter striped sweater that would make anyone else look like a fashion-challenged zebra. On Gwen, it not only worked. The entire outfit looked perfect.

Was her figure always that spectacular? Or had it simply evolved that way in direct, inverse proportion to Mary Jane's own plummeting self-esteem?

"Hi, Gwen. Um, can you move a little? I have to open my locker." She did everything in her power not to convey her real meaning, which was more along the lines of, "Can you move a little? Like into the rotating blades of a helicopter?"

"Oh, sure. Sorry." Gwen then scooted her hips, which gave MJ almost enough room to dial her lock combination. Almost. "Hey, I hear you were rescued by Spider-Man last night! That's so cool! Can you give me a few details? We're holding the *Gazette* for the story."

Mary Jane stopped spinning the lock, and for a moment she also stopped breathing.

Peter must have told her.

Peter must have called her up right after they spoke last night, way too late for anyone other than an intimate member of the opposite sex. Even Mary Jane, who had known Peter for years, and who was supposed to be his girlfriend, had had the decency to at least hesitate before calling a boy after eleven o'clock!

Before she jumped to any further appalling conclusions, she decided to ask a few questions. No need to totally freak herself out if there was a perfectly logical explanation. One that would rule out Peter phoning Gwen late at night, with a husky, love-soaked voice, using her near-mugging as an excuse to connect with her. No need to wig out until necessary.

165

"Oh, you heard about that," Mary Jane opened her locker with a little more force than necessary. She kept her tone casual. "Who told you?"

"Let's just say I have my sources," Gwen smiled.

Okay, now it was time to wig out.

"Peter?" Mary Jane spat the name as if it were a bundle of nails. "Peter told you?"

"No, he didn't." Gwen was quite a good little actress. She had just the right combination of surprise and hurt that would almost lead the unsuspecting to believe that, in fact, Peter had not told her.

"Yeah, right," MJ jammed her coat into the locker and pulled out a few of the books she needed.

"Really, he didn't. I can't believe he knew and didn't tell me," she said half to herself.

"You can drop the act, Gwen."

Gwen's wide, admittedly nicely made-up eyes were wide. "What are you talking about?"

"You and Peter. I'm not stupid."

"I never said you were!"

"Yeah, well. You just acted like it." She slammed the locker shut, causing a few passing students to stop and stare. "Just leave me alone, okay? You and Peter."

Then Mary Jane said something that would haunt her later, not only because it was so very untrue, but also because by even uttering the words, she felt a little piece of her soul chip away. "I hope you and Peter are very happy together."

The bell rang, and she turned to go to her English class. But she didn't. Instead, she went into the girls' bathroom, slipped into a stall, and cried.

Gwen stood motionless by Mary Jane's locker, an expression of stunned confusion on her face. Gradually, the confusion melted into placid contentment.

She couldn't wait to tell her friend Christina that she was right all along. Peter and Mary Jane had broken up!

Now maybe, at long last, Gwen Stacy had a chance!

* * *

To say that by the end of the day, Mary Jane Watson was in no mood to march around in circles to the soundtrack of My Fair Lady was a colossal understatement.

She saw Ms. Krumplesteater, whistle in mouth, clapping her hands off beat. "Okay, team! Let's dance!"

MJ stood motionless, watching the grim-faced chorus line up in place.

Why had she even come to rehearsal? She had a precious few hours between school and her job.

And then it hit her: She had to quit the play. There was no other option. She simply couldn't keep up with everything, and she needed to start taking on more shifts at work.

She would go home and write a note to Ms. Krumplesteater and Mr. Toby to explain the situation. That's exactly what she would do.

The decision made her feel miserable, knowing she would be letting everyone down, especially Wendy. But it wasn't as if she had a real choice.

Very slowly she backed out of the room, hoping to attract as little attention to herself as possible. Hoping nobody would notice she had even been there.

"Miss Watson?"

Drat. Foiled again.

"Oh, hello, Mr. Toby. I was just..."

"May I see you for a moment?"

Great. She knew what was coming: She was about to be booted from the musical anyway. Not that she didn't deserve the boot. Still, she hated it.

Just then she saw Wendy ambling over with a sly grin on her face. Wendy, her former best friend, had clearly defected to the dark side and joined the forces of evil.

And looking at Wendy, with those wonderful dimples, MJ missed her so much it hurt.

"Miss Watson, something has been brought to my attention," Mr. Toby began in his precise, overly enunciated stage-speak.

"Yes?" She tried not to look upset.

"I understand you have an extensive dance background."

Now *that* was unexpected. "Yes, I do. Um, I've studied with the Manhattan School of Ballet for years. I mean, not counting my stretch at Ruby's House-O-Dance."

"Would your training include any choreography? Specifically in the area of Broadway or modern dance, that sort of thing?"

"Sure. I choreographed the advanced class workshop recital to a Leonard Bernstein suite. I also reworked the dream sequence from *Oklahoma!* for four people, since that's all we had. I helped the junior movement class with their part in *The Music Man*. And I've..."

"And have you had any thoughts about the choreography in this show?"

She resisted the urge to say that in her mind, there *was* no choreography in the show. MJ thought for a moment. "I think I'd go with more organized dance movements, but not entirely in unison. More like the movie version. A few of the kids in the chorus can really dance, so I think they could do more ambitious steps. Sort of mini-solos, especially in the Covent Garden scenes. Belinda is an ex-cheerleader, and she can do amazing kicks. And Carl is on the gymnastics team — it's a total waste to have him just walk around. Oh, and a few groups could move slightly offbeat, in contrast to the major clusters. That would be so cool! Some of the more exuberant numbers could be incredible if we..."

"Enough!" Mr. Toby laughed, then he grew more serious. "I've watched you during the rehearsals, and have noticed that you sometimes do your own movements to the music. And frankly, they look terrific. Wendy here also brought you to my attention."

MJ looked over at Wendy, who nodded eagerly, as Mr. Toby continued. "Do you think you could help Ms. Krumplesteater with the musical? I know this is short notice. You understand, of course, that she will still be listed on the program as the choreographer. But can you be the assistant choreographer?"

"Oh, I'd love to! Really, I..." And then her voice softened as reality set in. "But, in all honesty, I don't think I can."

"And why, may I ask, not?"

"I have a job. And I need to keep that job for as long as, well. For as long as possible."

"Hm," he tapped his chin. "Let me see what I can come up with. We may be able to pay you a small salary. The PTA funds were allocated for the costumes and scenery, but we've managed to keep those costs way below budget. Maybe we can work something out."

"That would be so fantastic!" That might mean she wouldn't have to take extra spritzer shifts!

"But can you help Ms. Krumplesteater in the meantime?"

As if on cue, she blew the whistle and shouted "Okay, now about-face and walk in the other direction! Very good! One and a two and a..."

"Please?" Mr. Toby said with raised eyebrows. "Ms. Krumplesteater already knows we're asking you. And frankly, she's more anxious than anyone that this turns out well."

Wendy had remained quiet, but suddenly she spoke up. "You've gotta do this, MJ!"

"Okay, sure." She tried to sound calm, but the very thought of being able to work on the musical in this way was so incredibly exciting, she found it hard to stop smiling. "Great."

Wendy gave her a thumbs-up, and Mary Jane walked over to Ms. Krumplesteater. "Please tell me you're going to help out," she spoke from the side of her mouth, so as not to disturb the whistle.

"Yep. At least for now."

An expression of pure relief washed over the volley-ball coach, and she stepped back. "Okay, kids. Mary Jane Watson is going to help out with the choreography here. Do whatever she tells you."

With that Ms. Krumplesteater solemnly pulled a whistle on a purple lanyard from her pocket. "For you."

"Oh, thank you." Mary Jane leaned forward, and the coach slipped it over her head as if it were the French Medal of Honor. She half expected to be kissed on both cheeks.

She then turned to her fellow chorus members, their hopeful eyes bright and expectant.

"Well, let me see here," she began. "We'll start with some basic dance movements and build from there."

She had a lot to do. She needed to rent a copy of *My Fair Lady* from the video store, take notes, and get the CD so she could work out the dance numbers.

There was so much to do that she was almost overwhelmed.

She couldn't wait to get started.

* * *

By the time she got home from her spritzer girl job, she was too exhausted to dwell much on what had happened that day. Especially when it came to Peter.

There was homework to do, and some rough ideas to draft out about the show's choreography. She had to throw some clothes in the wash. Oh, and there was a quiz in — which class was it again?

The last thing she could think about was Peter Parker.

She picked up the phone and dialed.

"Hello?"

"Oh, hello, Mrs. Parker," she said to Peter's Aunt May. "This is Mary Jane. Is Peter in?"

"No, dear, he's not. He's off doing something or other on the school paper."

Thud.

"Great. Fine. Well, I should really be going now."

"I've been meaning to ask you, did you have a good time at the dance two weeks ago?"

Was it only two weeks ago?

"Yes. Yes we did. I did, anyway."

"You know, I never really saw the resemblance between Peter and his Uncle Ben until I saw him in Ben's tuxedo." Aunt May's voice wavered. "I honestly couldn't believe it."

Poor Aunt May. How lonely she must be. "And he's so like his uncle in character, too," she continued. "So strong and fine and good. So very loyal and true."

"I know," Mary Jane said softly. "Well, I'd better finish my homework now."

"Good night, dear."

"Good night."

She stared at the phone for a few moments, knowing who she really wanted to call next. Of course she shouldn't. It would be insane to make the next call. No good could possibly come of it.

And at the same time, she was dreading the fact that she would make the call. All she needed was to look a certain number up in the phonebook. Then...

Oh, look! There's the phonebook. Now, just page through until the right last name and...surprise! It's a listed number.

Without thinking further, she dialed the number.

A male answered. "Hey there, cutie-pie," the voice crooned. "I was just thinking about you."

"Excuse me?"

"You heard me, honeylips. I know it's you. Did you forget I've got caller ID?" He chuckled.

"Um, may I please speak to Gwen?"

There was a long pause. "Who is this?"

"I'm sorry," she said, flustered. "I must have the wrong number."

"No, wait." Now he sounded more normal. "May I ask who's calling?"

Weird! The low-voiced chuckling guy was coming off like someone's dad or something.

"This is Mary Jane Watson and..." Before she could say anything else, she heard the receiver being put down.

"Gwennie? Telephone. I think it's someone from school."

What was going on here?

"Hello," the dreadful voice said.

"Hi, Gwen. This is Mary Jane Watson."

A powerful silence. Then a noncommittal "Hi."

What she really wanted to ask was, Is Peter over there? And if so, why? And can you do me a favor and transfer to another school? Like in Montana?

Instead she said, "I'm sorry I was a little abrupt this morning."

Gwen's voice warmed. "No, I'm sorry I got all Lois Lane on you. You must have had a rough night."

Yeah, and you were most of the reason.

But MJ had figured out what to say before she made the call, just in case she actually got through. "It was a little rough. But it all happened so fast, one moment this guy in a ski mask was trying to get my purse. The next moment, Spider-Man was there."

"Wow. Do you mind if I write this down?"

"Sure. I mean, no, I don't mind. But if you have company or something," something like my boyfriend Peter, "I can call back later."

"Nope, no company here." Gwen didn't hear Mary Jane's sigh of relief. "What was he like?"

173

"Sort of tall, really mean eyes. It was hard to tell with the mask."

"Spider-Man?"

"No, the mugger!"

"Oh. What about Spider-Man? What was he like?"

"Well, he was fast. And he did look great in those tights."

"Tell me about it! I spent about an hour going over Peter's contact sheets just to check out his..." She cleared her throat. "Now, did he say anything to you?"

Mary Jane tried to ignore the mention of Peter. "Yep, he did. He said a few general things, like I should be more careful. And that...hey. That's a little odd."

"What's a little odd?"

"He told me I shouldn't be out so late on a school night."

"He said that?"

"Yeah. I didn't think much about it at the time, but I didn't say anything about being in school. Unless he just took one look and assumed I was a high school kid."

"But it was dark, right? I mean, if I saw you, even in daylight, I might just think you're about twenty-five or something."

"Really? That's so nice of you," Mary Jane couldn't help but be flattered.

"I'm totally serious. And especially at night. Oh, well. Anything else you remember?"

"He walked me to the bus stop."

"Get out! Are you kidding? Spider-Man walked you to the bus stop! Did he say anything?"

Mary Jane giggled a little. "He asked me if I had a fare card."

"No way! And what if you didn't have one — would he have pulled one out of his tights?"

"I have no idea! But you should have seen the look on the bus driver's face!"

They both laughed at the image, and then Mary Jane spoke. "Hey Gwen? Why are you so interested in Spider-Man?"

She took a deep breath. "I'm not sure. I mean, who is this guy? *What* is this guy? I think he's on the up-and-up, and that he's really a good person. But a lot of people, especially the police, think he's out for something. Like he's going to trick all of us into believing in him, and then do something terrible. Cops are always looking for the most cynical sort of angle."

"Why do you say that?"

Gwen gave a very unladylike snort. "Because my dad's a cop."

"Your dad's a cop!"

"Yep. He's a captain, actually."

"That's really cool." And as she spoke, suddenly it clicked into place. "Oh, my," was all she could say.

"Are you all right?"

"No, it's just that, well...does your dad go online much?"

"Yeah. He's a total computer nut. He even goes into these single-parent chat rooms. You know, 'how do I handle my troubled teen' stuff. Why?"

"No reason." Mary Jane thought she might be sick. Was it actually possible that her mother was dating Gwen Stacy's father?

Of all the millions of single guys out there, her mother found HIM?

"Can I ask you one last question?" Gwen said quietly.

She must know too! How could Mary Jane respond? She had to talk to her mother first, to make sure she wasn't mistaken. Still, she was pretty sure.

"What was your overall impression of him?" Gwen asked.

Of her dad? That he had a creepy voice and sounded like a lame game show host and...

"What do you mean?" Mary Jane's own voice went way too high.

"Spider-Man."

She sighed. Whew, close call. Then she refocused. "My overall impression?" She looked back on the night before, on all of her encounters with Spider-Man. And her perception of him was consistent. "I believe he's good."

"Good?"

"He has a good character. I really think he's strong and fine. Loyal and true."

Gwen sighed. "That's what I think, too. Try telling that to my dad, though."

I'll leave that to my mom, MJ thought.

But she said, "Well, I'd better get some homework done now."

"Yeah, me too. Hey, how did you do on that *Age of Innocence* quiz?"

Now Mary Jane smiled. "I aced it, thanks to you. Really, Gwen, I forgot to thank you. So thank you."

Gwen took a deep breath. "You're welcome. But I

need to thank you for the Midtown Makeover of the Year. Really, thank you for helping out that day."

"Anytime." Suddenly MJ didn't hate her so much. Then she added, "Hey, is Peter working late on some newspaper story or something?"

"No, not that I know of," Gwen answered. "Maybe it's for the *Bugle* and not the *Gazette*. The moonlighting creep. Bye. And thanks for the Spider-Man stuff. For everything."

"You're welcome. Bye."

Her mother was still awake. But Mary Jane was in no frame of mind to ask her about HotCop54's identity. In fact, she was in no mood to deal with anyone's real identity, be it Gwen or Peter, Spider-Man, or Wendy.

How did everything get so mixed-up?

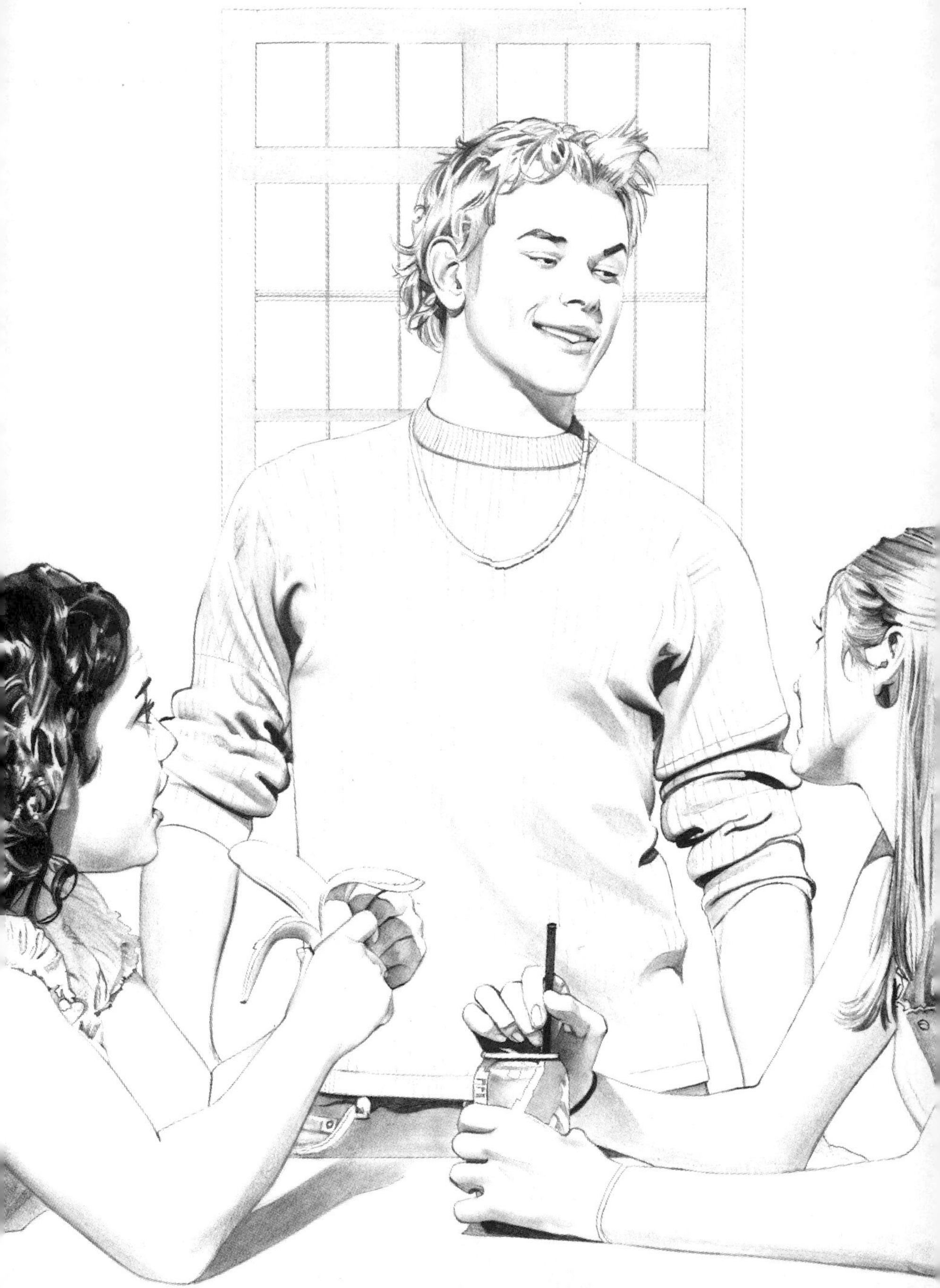

chapter 11

She heard him shout from down the hall. "Mary Jane. MJ!"

Her first reaction was to pretend she hadn't heard him. That was not only totally immature, but also impossible to ignore. At least a half dozen other kids were pointing him out.

"Hey, Mary Jane. Peter's calling."

"Peter wants you."

"Parker's yelping your name over there."

So she turned and smiled. "Hi."

"Hey. I hear you called last night."

Oh, no! He heard about her calling Gwen! She had to come up with a reasonable excuse.

"Well, you see I just thought..."

"Aunt May told you I was out?"

Aunt May. Aunt May! "Yes! She did. Sorry I called so late."

"What's up?"

"Nothing. I guess I don't remember what I called about."

"Oh, okay." He seemed a little disappointed. "Wendy told me about the stuff you're doing for the show. Sounds great."

"I hope I can do it. And I might even get paid."

"You'll be fantastic. You always are."

"Thanks."

"Listen, MJ. There's something I've been meaning to talk to you about. It's kind of serious."

He was going to make it official, to announce that he was now seeing Gwen.

"It's about Harry."

"I know. I've been expecting this," she said, then stopped. "Harry?"

"Yeah, Harry. I think he's hanging out with a rough crowd."

"Harry?"

"I was wondering if you can think of anything we can do for him. Something to help him along a bit."

"I'm not sure. Wow, Harry?" She thought about him, about how he seemed to have dropped out of sight. "Why do you think he's in trouble?"

"Well, it seems he's been going out late at night with those weird freshmen. I hear he may have been involved with stealing a couple of cars. That's just a rumor, of course."

"Stealing cars! Surely Harry can't be in on it." MJ was genuinely shocked.

"He's not the main force behind the plan, as I understand it. But he's the oldest, and the only one in that crew who can drive a car. I think those kids are smart enough to realize that if they ever got caught, Harry would take the fall."

"Oh, no. The poor guy, as if he hasn't had enough trouble already. I thought he seemed okay at the dance, though."

"Yeah, well, I thought so, too. But I think he was faking it."

"Pete, I can't help feeling guilty about this whole thing. I mean, I know we did what we had to do, but still. At the time I had no idea how much Harry would get hurt."

"That's exactly how I feel. So I was thinking." For the first time in the conversation Peter seemed slightly hesitant. "Well, how would you like to do something with him?"

"Just me and Harry?"

"No, no. Maybe the four of us."

"Four?"

"You, me, Harry and Gwen. I think he likes her. Does that sound fun?"

"Sure. It's my dream date. But I've been really busy and..."

"Great! I'll get back to you with details."

And then, just as quickly as he appeared, he was gone, leaving her to wonder — who was he hoping his date was going to be, her...or Gwen?

* * *

Finally, Harry had a solid reason for talking to Gwen Stacy.

"Gwen." He came up to her in the lunchroom.

"Oh, hi, Harry. What's up?"

"Guess who I met up with last night?"

She had also heard the rumors about Harry and his emerging career as a criminal. "I haven't the faintest idea."

"None other than your hero, Spider-Man!"

"Get outta town!" She pushed his shoulder, which pleased him more than he cared to admit even to himself. "What happened?"

He knew she was going to ask that very question, and he had an answer prepared.

"I was coming home late from the library, and he just stopped to chat."

In reality, Harry and his new gang had been trying steal another car. He felt miserable about it. The money meant nothing to him. Worse than nothing, it was a hideous reminder of what he had done. And just the other day he learned his trust fund would be unfrozen by the end of the week.

He didn't tell the gang that soon he'd have his own money back. After all, then he would be as much of a target as any parked car. He also failed to mention that he handed all of his car money to a local soup kitchen to rid himself of the guilt. (It hadn't worked.)

But he couldn't seem to get away from those kids. And then last night, out of nowhere Spider-Man swooped down. The younger guys scattered, and Harry would have as well. But for some reason Spider-Man stuck to Harry, telling him to go home. Telling him that he would ruin his life if he continued doing those things. The usual garbage.

But he couldn't very well tell Gwen all those things. So he reduced the tale to the library story.

"You were coming home late from the library." Gwen fumbled in her backpack for a paper and pencil. "Mind if I write this down?"

"Not at all," he said seriously.

"Okay, which library were you coming home from?" She stared at him, pencil poised.

Which library? There was more than one?

Maybe he should have thought this out a little better.

"The library by the park," he smiled, shoving his hands into his pants pockets.

"By the park? Which park?"

"Oh, you know. The big one."

"The Forest Hills library?"

"That's the one!"

"Okay, what time was it?"

"Late. It was real late, because I was studying so hard. You know, and looking at all the books they have there."

"I know," she nodded. "That's a great library."

"Isn't it? I just love that place."

"So what time was it, exactly?"

"Oh, let me see. I guess it was about one in the morning. Give or take."

"One in the morning? But the library closes at nine!"

"It does? I mean, it does. Yes. I am aware of that." Think, Harry. THINK. "But I was so upset at having to leave that I went over to that all-night diner."

"Which one?"

"The one that's open all night. They serve coffee and stuff."

"The one off Continental?"

"That's the one!"

"They have great doughnuts there. Especially the glazed ones. So anyway, you were in the diner. And then what happened?"

"Um, I was in the diner." He nodded his head. "Eating glazed doughnuts. And drinking coffee. Then I left and that's when I saw Spider-Man."

"Wait a minute." She scribbled in her notebook. "So you were drinking coffee and eating doughnuts for four hours?"

"Yep. I really like those doughnuts." He looked off into the distance, as if the answers he needed would be just beyond the horizon. Or at least through the lunchroom doors. "Especially the glazed."

"You must. And then?" She leaned forward, encouraging him to continue.

"Well, then I left to go home. And that's when I met up with Spider-Man."

"Cool! And what did he say?"

"Well, he just came up and said, 'Hi, Harry. How are the doughnuts tonight?' And I said, 'Very good, Spider-Man.'"

"So he knows your name?"

"What?"

"Spider-Man knows your name?"

Harry stood for a moment with his mouth open. And then he realized with a jolt that Spider-Man *did* know his name! Just before he grabbed the back of his jacket to get him away from the car, he had said, "Harry! Are you out of your mind?"

"He does," Harry said with some wonderment. "He called me by my name. Wow, that's really cool."

"Totally cool." Gwen looked up at Harry and smiled.

"Yeah," Harry nodded with a grin. "And he just said a few things. Oh, and he did say I shouldn't be out so late on a school night."

"He said that?"

"Yep."

"Interesting." Gwen flipped through her notes, then tapped her pencil. "Harry, do you think Spider-Man is a good guy?"

"You mean good guy, versus a bad guy?"

"Yes. I'm trying to figure him out, to determine if he's trying to help or if he's just..."

"He's a good guy," Harry said without hesitation. "Seriously. It's like he cares or something. Like he knows who you are, and wants you to be safe. But he also wants you to do the right things for yourself."

"So in the end, how would you describe Spider-Man?"

Harry thought for a moment, and when the realization hit him, he was every bit as surprised as Gwen was. "A friend."

"A friend?"

"Yes. I felt as if he was a friend of mine. Wow, that's it. He's a genuine friend."

"Harry, is there..."

"Um, listen, Gwen. I'm sorry, I really have to go." Harry seemed inexplicably upset. "Sorry."

He walked out of the lunchroom, leaving Gwen to look over her notes.

Who *was* this guy, this Spider-Man?

* * *

Finally something was going right!

Mary Jane had stayed up late the night before, watching the My Fair Lady video and jotting down ideas. And then somehow, during the school day, more ideas kept coming to her. Images of how a dance would look on stage, of how certain chorus members would look doing this movement, or that step.

She knew enough about the physical abilities and limitations of the other dancers to know what they could and could not do. And with an absolute, glorious certainty, she realized that the finished product could be spectacular!

It was even better when she got to rehearsal. She began to block the Covent Garden dance sequence, based a little on the movement she had seen in the video. But based a lot on her own imagination and the space they would have on the Midtown High stage.

"Okay," she clapped. "Belinda, you are here. This table will be a bushel, I checked with the stage manager. And in the center will be a flower cart, which will have wheels so we can move it around during the number..."

Ms. Krumplesteater was wonderful. It was an odd shift, but gradually throughout the practice, she became Mary Jane's assistant, instead of the other way around. And she was fantastic! Mr. Toby came by and watched for a while, his expression unreadable. Even though Mary Jane was slightly distracted by his presence, she didn't let it disturb her.

This was something she could do. She knew dance, and knew it well.

"Miss Watson, may I please see you for a moment?"

It was during a five-minute break, and a feeling of dread clenched in her stomach.

"Please," she thought to herself. "Please don't take this away."

When she got close enough, Mr. Toby spoke quietly. "Miss Watson, I'm afraid I have some bad news."

No, please. Please let me do this.

"Yes?" She patted her face with a towel.

"Well." Then he smiled. "First the good news: You are doing a magnificent job! Good grief, even in one afternoon I can't believe the change in the chorus! And I can see it in their faces, too! Bravo, Miss Watson."

She swallowed. "Thank you. But what's the bad news?"

The smile fell from his face. "I'm afraid I looked into the PTA funds. And since you are only a student, and officially the assistant choreographer, without teaching credentials, of course...."

This was it. She would have to give this up, work the double spritzing shifts. She held the towel tightly in her fist.

"...we can only give you four hundred and fifty dollars. I am so sorry. But on the bright side, we will give you this money now, in cash. Otherwise it will get eaten up by some other group. And believe me, at this point we need you more than we need more green paint."

Did she hear right?

"I'm sorry, what did you just say?"

He pulled a folded envelope from his jacket pocket. "It's only four hundred and fifty dollars, but..."

But he didn't have a chance to finish. Mary Jane reached up and kissed him on the cheek.

"Oh, Mr. Toby! You have no idea what this means, no idea at all!" She was perilously close to crying. But that was okay. The theater people were always crying.

"Yes, I do know what it means. It means this production has a fighting chance of being everything I dreamed it could be."

"Thank you, thank you!" He handed her the envelope, and she did everything in her power to resist the urge to kiss that, too. "And can I use your office phone? I have to make a quick call! Maybe two."

"Local?"

"Absolutely!" She needed to call Mr. Tiller to inform him that she could no longer be a spritzer girl. And then she needed to call her mother, to inform her that the money would hers within a few hours.

After making the joyous calls, Mary Jane returned to the rehearsal. And after it ended, everyone in the chorus, even Ms. Krumplesteater, agreed that it was the best rehearsal ever.

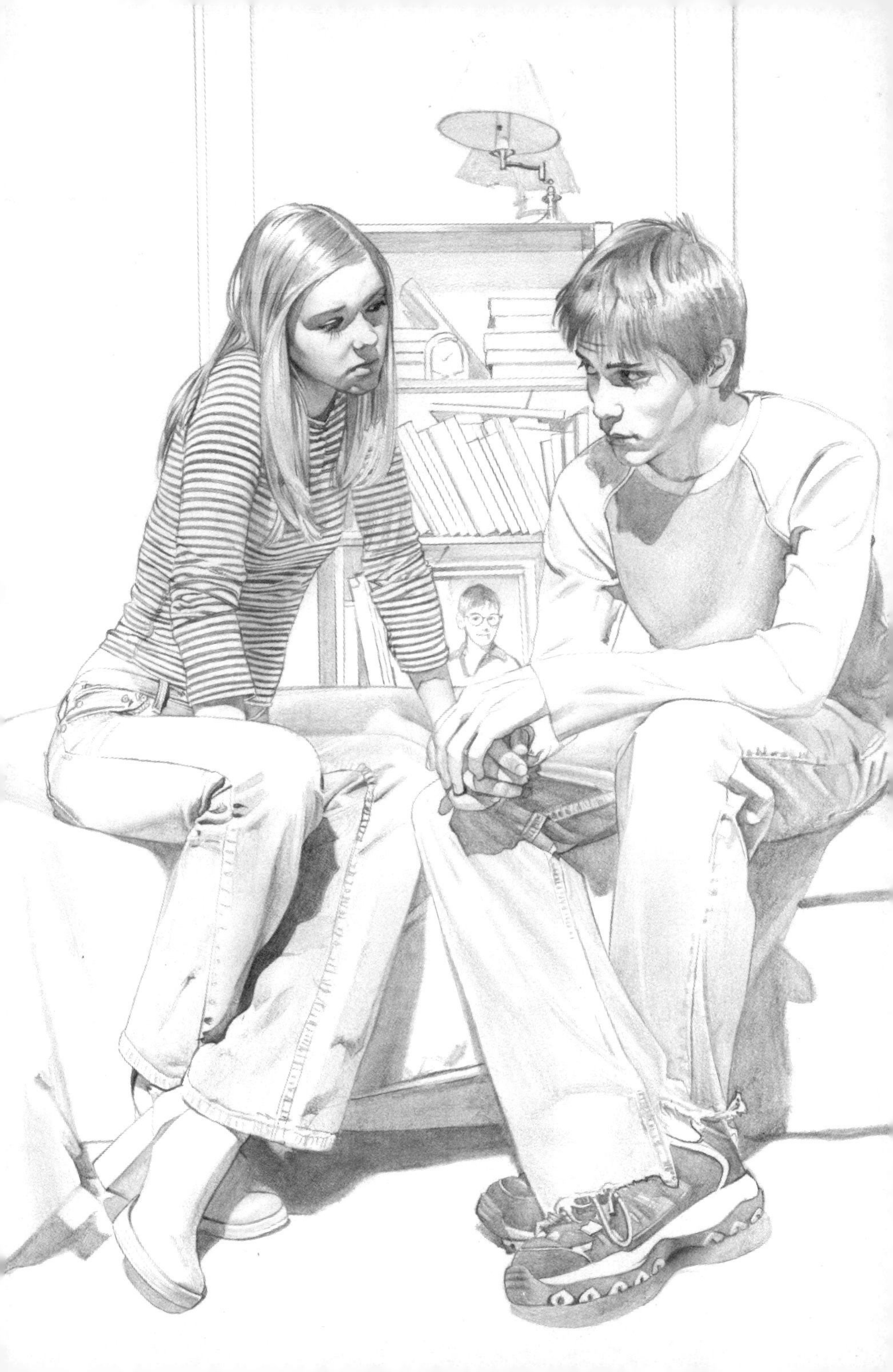

chapter 12

Mr. Tiller had not been thrilled to hear that one of his perfume girls was leaving the Grimby family. But he was not terribly surprised either. "Seasonal work," he moaned. "It's always the same." And he even promised to mail her the check for her last few shifts.

Madeline Watson *was* thrilled, however. This meant at least for the next month, rent would be paid — and on time! But it wasn't just the money that excited her — it was also the fantastic opportunity for Mary Jane to show off her work in the musical. She hugged her daughter the moment she walked through the door.

"Oh, honey, I'm so proud of you! You really deserve this."

"Thanks! I'm really psyched, too." She hugged her mom back.

"I hope this gets you out of that little depression you've been in," her mom added, giving her back a final pat.

"Excuse me?" MJ stepped back.

"You know. Your little funk."

"What do you mean?"

"Sweetie, you're transparent as glass. And I just have a feeling, well," Madeline Watson smiled sadly. "Whatever is bothering you runs very deep."

Mary Jane's shoulders sagged a little. "Oh, Mom. There have been so many things. The money situation..."

"Which will be resolved," Madeline replied firmly. "I have three more job interviews tomorrow. We will be fine, and now, with this…." She held up the envelope with the money. "Well, let's just say you bought us the time we need."

"So you don't think we'll have to move?"

"No, I don't, honey. A few days ago, I wasn't so sure. But now, things are really looking up. And do you realize that thanks to your help, I'll be paying rent three days early this month?"

"Yeah, well. My help wouldn't have been needed if I hadn't borrowed the money from Mrs. Stevens in the first place."

"I would have done the exact same thing in your situation," her mother said kindly. "The more I think about it, the more certain I am of it."

"Thanks," she sighed. "But, well. There's that. And also things are not so great with me and Wendy. Or me and Peter, for that matter."

"I've had a hunch. What's up with Wendy?"

"I don't know. She's all into the theater crowd now, this tight little clique. It's like they don't want to wander too far from their mother ship or something. As if they will all be contaminated by the non-theater people. And that's who Wendy was, before she got the part."

"Insecurity," her mom stated.

"Huh?"

"Insecurity. That's the basis for most cliques. Insecurity. Especially theater people. Trust me on this, I was one of them myself."

"You're joking?"

"Nope. Why do you think I moved up to New York in the first place?"

"I always thought it was to be with Daddy."

"Well, that was part of it. But mainly it was because I wanted to see if I could make it as an actress up here. I tried really hard, Mary Jane. And was rejected over and over again. That's what theater people go through on a regular basis, even in high school."

"It's a lot like ballet," MJ thought about all the dancers she knew. How worried they were about gaining weight, about the next new dancer, about getting hurt, and especially about snagging the best role in the next ballet.

"It's exactly like ballet. And Wendy, like everyone else, is insecure."

"Not about her talent." Mary Jane waved her hand in the air. "I mean, you should hear her. She's amazing."

"Especially about her talent. Come on, Mary Jane. Look at the situation — here Wendy came seemingly out of nowhere and got the lead role in *My Fair Lady*. How many other girls tried out for that part?"

"Including me?"

"Including you."

"Well, I guess about...wow. About fifty, maybe more."

"Think of that! And now she has to prove herself every day in front of kids who've have been doing Summerstock since they were six. In front of all the other talented girls who tried out for the same part and didn't get it," her mother added. She leaned forward and smiled. "Get it?"

She had never thought of it like that before! She'd just assumed Wendy's distance had been all her fault somehow. "I get it! Oh, poor Wendy! And when I wasn't there reassuring her every two seconds that she was fantastic, she must have assumed I thought it was because she was no good. Or that I was jealous."

"Exactly."

"And on top of that, it was Wendy who told the director of the show about my dance background."

"Right. And just think, you've been wasting all this time thinking you've lost your best friend, when in truth, you've never had a better friend."

"I've gotta call Wendy right now!"

"Great," her mother laughed as MJ ran to the phone. "And then you can get ready for tonight."

"For tonight?"

"Yep. We're all going out to dinner."

"We?"

"I've told you this three times. We're meeting my boyfriend and his daughter for dinner at that cute new Tiki restaurant around the corner."

Wonderful, she thought. Just because she was feeling slightly better about Gwen didn't mean she was ready to break bread with her. Or whatever it is they ate in Hawaii. In fact, she could think of nothing she'd rather do less than eat dinner with her mother's new boyfriend and his daughter, who also happened to be her own boyfriend's new girlfriend. Ugh.

She forced her most pleasant face and gritted her teeth. "Great!" And then she called Wendy.

* * *

"It's really great to meet you," Captain George Stacy stood and shook Mary Jane's hand.

"Great," was all she could reply, her teeth still clenched.

He was tall, taller than she expected. Not that she had been expecting much. But he was tall and sort of attractive, if you liked older guys with mustaches. And he was wearing a sports jacket that looked, well, nice, if not slightly out of place among the kitschy, grass-hut decor of the restaurant.

Gwen was sitting in a chair with her arms crossed. "Hi," she said to both Madeline and Mary Jane.

"Hi." Mary Jane began to take a seat between Madeline and Captain Stacy, but her mother gently guided her to the other seat, next to Gwen. Captain Stacy held the chair for her mother and, she noticed, rubbed her back just a little before he returned to his own place.

"Why, Gwen. Your father has told me how pretty you are, but honestly, he didn't do you justice," her mother gushed.

"Thanks," Gwen said with only a quick glance at her mom.

"Well, in all honesty we have your daughter to thank for that, Maddy," Captain Stacy passed the bright red menus to MJ and her mom.

Maddy? No one ever called her mother Maddy! She hated it!

Mary Jane looked at her mother and waited for the spark of anger that name invariably evoked. There was a spark all right. But it sure wasn't anger.

"What do you mean, Georgie?" She batted her eyes.

Gwen stiffened and shot her father a questioning look. He chuckled. "It's okay, Gwennie. I don't mind it when Maddy calls me Georgie. But if anyone at the station house calls me that, well. That's another thing entirely." Then he turned to MJ's mother.

"Your daughter, it seems, helped Gwen out with her makeup and all those girl things I don't know anything about."

"You did?" Her mother seemed incredibly pleased. "Why, that was nice of you. And Gwen, I must admit, you look wonderful."

"Thanks," Gwen said, taking a sudden interest in the menu, which looked like it was laminated onto a flattened piece of coconut bark. A waiter in chinos and a Hawaiian shirt came by to take their drink orders.

Captain Stacy cleared his throat. "As I was saying, it was tough raising Gwennie on my own. You know, as a man. And as a man who puts in a lot of hours on the job. I just don't know anything about the girlie stuff."

"Oh, Ricky," her mother patted his hand. And for a moment they just sat there holding hands and staring at each other.

Mary Jane thought she might get sick.

"Anyone want to share a pupu platter?" Gwen shouted.

"Yeah, I do," Mary Jane overlapped.

"Great."

And again there was silence, while their parents grinned like a couple of dizzy puppies.

"Anyone want tea?" Mary Jane grabbed the pot.

"Yeah, I do." Gwen pushed her cup towards MJ, who dribbled some tea in a circle around the bamboo cup before making actual contact. "Dad? Tea."

He pulled his eyes away from Maddy for a moment and handed his cup to Mary Jane. She came close to scalding his hand, but his quick movements spared his right hand from third-degree burns. She splashed some tea in his cup.

"Mom? Tea." Madeline raised both of her hands from the table, and out of his grasp, to avoid a similar fate.

"Well, I see where Mary Jane gets her grace," he said without a hint of irony.

Gwen snorted.

"So Gwen," Madeline began fresh. "I hear you are the editor of the school newspaper. How exciting that must be!"

"Yeah. It's pretty cool."

"Mary Jane, doesn't Peter work for the newspaper, too?"

Mary Jane had a sudden urge to dive under the table. "Yeah."

Madeline brightened, "So you know Peter? Such a sweet boy. Mary Jane has known him since elementary school. Honey, what was that name they called him at Bradford?"

"Pukey Parker." She was unable to resist smiling. "He threw up during a third grade assembly."

"Ouch," Gwen grinned back. "That had to hurt."

"Parker, Parker. Why does that name ring a bell?" Captain Stacy frowned. "Oh, wait a minute, isn't he related to Ben Parker, the guy who was murdered a few months back?"

"That was his uncle," Mary Jane said quietly. "Uncle Ben. Now he just lives with his Aunt May."

"That's sad," Captain Stacy looked at his daughter.

"It's even worse," Madeline added. "His parents were killed when he was a young boy. When was that, Mary Jane?"

"Fourth grade. We were in fourth grade." The memory came back to her, of that terrible day in school when Peter was called out of class. Of his parents' funeral, of how sad and small Peter had looked at the grave.

"Wow," Gwen said, looking at Mary Jane. "I had no idea. He never said a word about that. I always wondered why he lived with his aunt and uncle."

"Well, that's why." Mary Jane took a sip of tea. "They were wonderful people, the Parkers."

"Yes, Mary Jane spent quite a lot of time over at their house, didn't you? Dr. Parker helped you and Peter with a science project that year. He was an awfully nice boy, even back then. And didn't he go to some of your dance recitals?"

"Yes, Mom. He did."

Gwen nodded slowly. "You two really go way back, don't you?"

"I guess we do. Yes."

Madeline and George, a.k.a. Maddy and Georgie, were speaking softly to each other. Her mother was smiling, and he was staring intently.

"Do you think if we hosed them down with cold water, they'd calm down?" Gwen asked under her breath.

Unexpectedly, Mary Jane laughed. Their parents didn't notice. "I seriously doubt it."

Gwen took a deep breath. "Listen, Mary Jane. I'm really sorry. I mean, I guess you know I've had a crush on Peter for a long time."

"Really?" She feigned surprise, but not very convincingly.

"Yeah, really. But you are his girlfriend. I mean, I wish..." Gwen fumbled with her teacup.

"You wish what?"

"I wish I could be more like you. There. I said it."

"What?" Mary Jane thought she must have heard wrong.

"Oh, come on. I'd never have a chance next to someone like you. You're gorgeous, you..."

"Shut up!"

"Seriously. Everything you do, you do well. You were a cheerleader. You're the choreographer for the musical. You're smart and popular.

"Everything about you seems so perfect, y'know?" Gwen continued. "Honestly, if you weren't so nice, I think I'd hate you."

"Well, what about you? Why do you think I've been so jealous? Peter always says how smart you are, how funny. That you're a great writer, and really know how to run a newspaper."

"He says that?" She smiled. "Well, forget about it when it comes to you. He talks about you all the time. It's 'Mary Jane' this and 'Mary Jane says that' or 'once Mary Jane did such and such.'"

"He says those things?" Mary Jane felt a warm rush go through her. "Thank you for telling me."

"What I really envy is that you know exactly who you are."

Mary Jane thought she was joking. "Yeah, right."

"Seriously. I mean, no guy ever looked at me before you helped me with my makeup and all that. I don't know who the heck I am — smart chick? Hot chick wannabe? Somewhere in-between? Take your pick. But you know exactly who you are. You're so confident."

"No, I'm not," was all she could say. Somehow she was both touched and flattered by Gwen's honesty.

"It's true."

They were both quiet for a moment. Then MJ had a thought. "Hey, what about you and Harry Osborn? I saw you guys dancing at the Winter Formal." She leaned closer. "He's really cute. And he's actually a really good guy, once you get to know him. He's just been having a hard time since his dad got arrested."

"Arrested?" Captain Stacy asked.

"He can hear anything, and usually does, especially when it involves work," moaned Gwen. "I wasn't talking to you, Dad."

"Are you talking about Norman Osborn's son?" he continued. "Harry. Right. Nice kid, I saw him at the arraignment. Not hanging with the best company these days, though."

"Harry?" Gwen asked.

"Yep. I've heard a few things here and there at the precinct."

"Spider-Man," Gwen said.

"What?" her dad asked.

"He said he met up with Spider-Man the other night after leaving the library."

"Harry at the library?" Mary Jane questioned. "What, was there some sort of retrospective on swimsuit models or something?"

Captain Stacy laughed once, then stopped when his daughter glared. "Well," he said in a serious, businesslike tone. "I'll keep an eye out for him. Maybe have a little talk with him."

"Dad, please!"

"No, Gwen," Mary Jane said in a rush. "That might really help him. I mean, his dad is away. He really needs some guidance. That would be really great, Captain Stacy."

Just then the waiter reappeared. Gwen and MJ both asked for the pupu platter at the same time, and both later admitted they loved to order it mainly because it was so fun to say pupu in a restaurant.

Their parents shared a Lover's Jade Delight. Mary Jane couldn't remember seeing her mother so happy, and Captain Stacy was acting like a smitten teenager.

And by the end of the meal, both Gwen and Mary Jane agreed that maybe, just maybe, their parents dating might not be such a bad thing after all.

* * *

"Hi, Peter. It's Mary Jane. Sorry to be calling so late."

"It's not that late," she could hear the smile in his voice. "I'm glad you called. What's up?"

"I hate to ask you this, but could you come over?"

"Now?"

"As soon as possible."

"Sure. I'll be right there."

Somehow Peter managed to make it over to Mary Jane's place within minutes.

"That didn't take long," she said as she opened the door.

"The bus was right there," he walked in and took off his scarf and jacket. "And there wasn't much traffic. Oh, hi, Mrs. Watson."

Her mother walked out of the kitchen. "Hello, Peter. Why, we were just talking about you tonight."

"Who was?" Peter looked slightly alarmed.

"Just me and Mary Jane. And Gwen Stacy."

Now Peter looked as if he might faint. "Gwen Stacy? How on earth..."

"And Captain Stacy," Madeline concluded.

"Captain Stacy?" he said in a rasp.

"You know, Gwen's dad. The cop."

"What, was someone arrested or something?"

"Worse. Mom and Captain Stacy are, well," she nudged Peter. "You know."

It took a moment for the information to sink in, and a slow dawning smile spread across his face. "Oh, I see! He's a great guy, Mrs. Watson."

"You can call her Maddy," MJ said breezily.

"You two," Madeline Watson giggled. "Really! I'm going to go read, but there's some tea and oatmeal cookies in the kitchen."

"Thanks, Mom."

"Thanks, Mrs. Watson," Peter chimed in. When she closed her door, he looked at MJ, dumbstruck. "You've got to be joking — your mom's seeing Gwen's father?"

"Yep. And it's not that bad. Want some tea?"

They went into the kitchen and she motioned to the table.

"Peter, I haven't been honest with you." She took a cookie from the plate, then put it down.

"You haven't?"

She passed the plate to him, and he shook his head no.

"What haven't you been honest about?"

Mary Jane closed her eyes for a moment, wondering where to even begin. Then she felt his warm hand cover hers.

She opened her eyes, and he was looking at her intently. And for the first time she realized he was nervous, apprehensive. Even frightened. Somehow, that made her relax.

"Peter, I was incredibly jealous of Gwen Stacy."

"What?" There was a shadow of a smile on his face.

"I thought you were going to dump me for her."

The smile vanished. "Mary Jane, why would you ever think that? Did I say anything, or do anything to indicate that?"

"No, not really. You said she was funny and smart and really knows her way around a newspaper."

"Yeah? And?"

"Well, I guess that was it."

"I said the same thing about Charlie Foy and Adam Katz, and that never bothered you."

"But they aren't hot chicks."

"That's what you think. Charlie Foy happens to have great legs."

"Peter, I'm serious."

"Sorry," he held her hand tighter. "But Mary Jane, that thought never crossed my mind."

"She has a crush on you, though."

"No, she doesn't."

"Yes, she does. She told me tonight over dinner."

"Remind me to go out to dinner with you more often," he smiled. "What's wrong?"

"There's another thing I haven't been honest about."

And then she told him the whole saga of Le Petite Araignee, of discovering the truth about the prices. Of meeting with Mrs. Stevens in the bathroom, borrowing the money. And of the trouble with her mother and the finances. Of having to take a job, which kept her from Peter as well as ballet. She explained all of it.

"That's why I had to get that stupid job at Grimby's. That's why I've been so tired and grumpy."

"Why didn't you tell me this before?" He shook his head in disbelief.

"Because I thought you'd be hurt."

"I *am* hurt. Hurt that you didn't trust me enough to tell me about all of this. Come on, Mary Jane, we would have thought of something that night. The two of us together? We would have been fine."

"Wouldn't your masculine pride have been wounded?"

He let out a deep breath. "Mary Jane, it's me. Pukey Parker."

"But there was more than that. I know how tough things have been financially for you and Aunt May. You said Aunt May sometimes cries over the utility bills. She would never stop sobbing if she ever saw the dinner bill."

"Mary Jane," he began.

"And also..."

"Let me finish." He put a finger lightly on her lips. "We know each other too well to hide things. And I really believe that the only reason there ever is to hide something is if there is a certainty that the other person will, indeed, be hurt by the information."

"But that's exactly what I thought!"

"No, I mean really hurt, as in physical harm. Not just pride or feelings."

"Great. So if I ever decide to become a gangster, you won't get pissed at me if I don't tell you, is that it?"

He didn't smile. "Sort of."

A chill went up her spine. Suddenly she wanted to know. She needed to know. "Peter, the other night when I was mugged," she began.

Peter took a cookie. "Hey, where's that tea?"

"Oh, over here. As I was saying..."

She poured him a cup and put she sugar bowl and creamer in front of him. "Aren't you having any tea?"

"Nah," she shook her head. "Gwen and I drank about three pots of tea tonight at the restaurant. But Peter, what I was wondering is..."

"Mary Jane? How could the bill have been that high?"

She paused, then sat down. "I guess because Gwen and I had the pupu platter and that's always expensive, but really it wasn't too bad and..."

"No, no," he poured milk into his tea and stirred. "At Le Petite Araignee. Even taking into consideration all the wildly expensive things you ordered..."

"I ordered?"

He pretended to be looking over a menu. "'Oh, I'll have the Dover sole and the truffles and the white asparagus and is the lobster out of season? Then I simply must have it!'"

"Was I that bad?" She cringed.

"Worse, but you were cute. Anyway, there is no way that would reach over four hundred dollars."

"I know, that's the thing. We got the wrong bill. Or they added stuff to ours." She got up and returned with the torn original check, and the Xerox copies she had made.

"Who tore this up?"

"They did. I went back the next day and the main waiter guy did this."

Peter looked up at her. Wow, she thought. Had his eyes become even more blue?

"Two bottles of wine," he whistled through his teeth. "After dinner drinks? The brandy must have been yours. It's eighteen dollars and out of season."

"Very funny," she smiled.

"So what did they say when you came back?"

"They said we paid in cash, and that we must have been there and eaten all that. So there was nothing to be done."

"They remembered you? Us?"

"Yeah. I mean, they pretended not to, but they did. Especially the guy who gave us the free sodas."

"That guy why saw me play basketball?"

"Yeah, why?"

"Mary Jane, do you realize if they say we had all this," he held up the copy, "that means they served liquor to minors? And I mean a lot of liquor?"

"So...wait a moment. That's illegal!"

"Bingo!"

"What are we going to do?"

"My dear, I think you just gave me my first real article for the *Daily Bugle*. How does this sound: 'Top Restaurant Serves Booze to Minors!'"

"Or how about: 'Top Restaurant Guilty of Age Discrimination and Fraud!' That's just as bad."

Suddenly he stood up and took a couple of cookies. "I'm off to write up a few pitches." He leaned down and kissed her. "Are you okay?"

"Yeah," she smiled. "I'm great."

Grabbing his coat and scarf, he smiled. "You sure are."

It wasn't until later, after he left, that she realized she never had the chance to ask him about Spider-Man. And on further thought, she realized he never gave her the chance to ask.

Interesting.

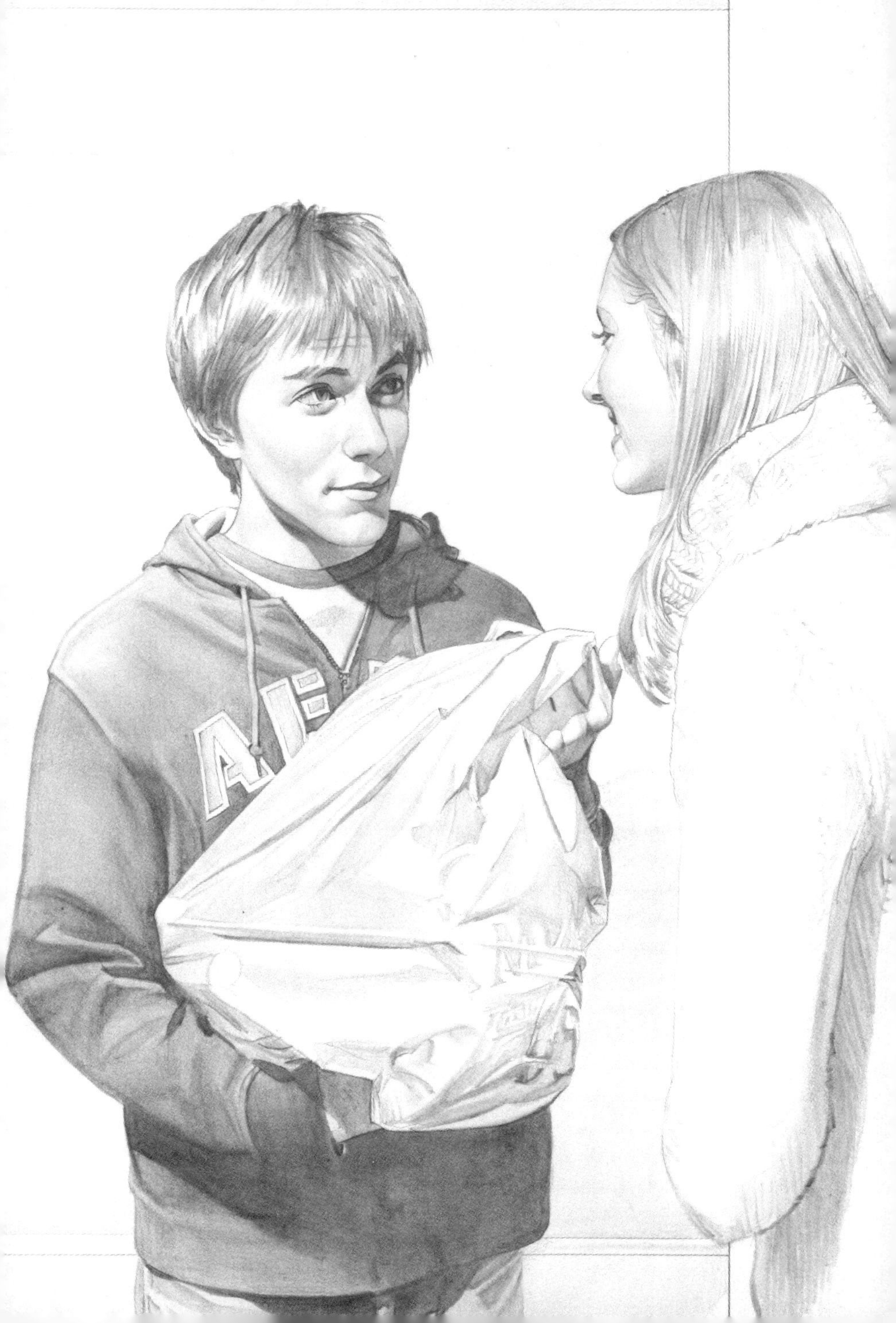

chapter 13

Mary Jane came home from school a few days later to find her mother sitting in the living room, a stunned expression on her face, smoking a cigarette.

It could only mean one thing — the landlord kicked them out of the apartment.

"Mom?"

Madeline Watson jumped. "Mary Jane. I wasn't expecting you so soon. Don't you have rehearsal tonight?"

"Not tonight. The tech crew needs the space to finish some of the bigger pieces of scenery. What's wrong?"

"Oh, Mary Jane, I don't know what I'm going to do!"

So this was it. They would have to find a new place to live.

"It's okay. I can get another job and..."

"Honey, I have a job."

"You what? You mean we're not leaving this apartment?"

Her mother looked at her as if she had suddenly gone mad. "What are you talking about?"

"I just thought that..."

"No, no. Norma Bates from Skye Bleu just called, and I'm to be the East Coast makeup consultant. They want me to help develop new lines, and to come up with new applications. I'll be making twice the salary I was before." She paused to take a deep breath. "There is no way I can do this."

"Of course you can!" Mary Jane laughed. "Mom, you'll be perfect! But how did this happen? I thought you were fired!"

"I was." She snubbed out her cigarette. "Then it seems Mrs. Horton Stevens heard about it, and started a grassroots campaign to get my job back. She had all of her Upper East Side friends, women with names on the society page, calling to say they would boycott all Skye Bleu products unless I was rehired immediately. Oh, and then this came in the mail today."

She went over to the table by the door and picked up a pale blue envelope of linen stationary. From it she pulled out a crisp one hundred dollar bill. "She said she was mistaken. She only lent you four hundred the night at Le Petite Araignee. She found the other hundred dollar bill in her coat pocket. Can you imagine? I guess a hundred dollar bill is like change in the couch cushions to Mrs. Horton Stevens."

"Mom, this is fantastic!"

"But I can't do this job, I can't. I don't have the experience."

"Yes, you are, Mom. Who's more qualified than you to consult on makeup? You were a beauty queen. You've been a stage actress. And you've been the Skye Bleu Salesgal of the Month twice."

Slowly Madeline Watson smiled.

"Maybe I can do this," she began. "I was thinking just the other day that what they need is an upscale line, something with really high-end packaging. And if they could come out with better contour brushes, with finer bristles..."

Without a word Mary Jane pulled out a notebook and pen and handed it to her mother.

"I can do this," her mother said as she began scribbling down her ideas. "I *can* do this."

* * *

The *Daily Bugle* was delighted with Peter's idea, and even gave him a small expense account so that Peter and Mary Jane could go to other pricey restaurants and order dinner and a glass of wine.

"No Dover sole," he warned before they hit their first place.

But it was amazing how many restaurants served them, even when they purposely dressed more as their real teenage selves. Peter would go back the next day to interview the staff and owners, and was even offered bribes by a few of the places.

A few times they went with Gwen and Harry, who seemed to be having a good time together. Occasionally Mary Jane would see the way Gwen looked at Peter, that vague longing she recognized so well in herself. But it no longer bothered her. For now, at least, she was sure of herself, and of Peter.

And in the meantime, Spider-Man continued his crime sweep of the entire city. But the more thugs he managed to snag, the more annoyed the police, and even the major newspapers, seemed to grow. There were editorials demanding that he unmask himself. "What does he have to hide?"

Politicians were suspicious, because he seemed to be the one guy no one could control. What was he really after?

One afternoon, a week or so before *My Fair Lady* opened, Peter stopped by rehearsal. Mary Jane was busy work-

211

ing with Wendy on the ballroom dance sequence, but she stepped outside to speak to him.

"Are you okay?"

"Yeah," he said, clearly agitated. "I mean no. This is so messed up." He was not at all himself, his eyes wide and unfocused. "I just went by the *Bugle* offices to turn in the write-up from last weekend, and I heard that two of the guys Spider-Man caught are being set free."

"Why?"

"Because they found themselves a lawyer who said their civil rights had been violated. They claim they never intended to rob that old lady with her shopping cart. They claim they were going to help her across the street."

"Yeah, right! Didn't these two guys have a long list of prior arrests?"

"The lawyer says that has nothing to do with this case. According to him, Spider-Man attacked them first! You should have seen these guys, MJ, they were just looking for an easy target, and this little old lady... I mean, she could have been anyone. She could have been Aunt May."

She cocked her head slightly.

"I'm just so..." He made a fist. "This is so messed up. Spider-Man really tries to make a difference and catch the bad guys. But then the system fails, and the bad guys still get off. It's not supposed to be like this."

"Peter," she reached up and turned his face towards her. Suddenly he seemed to relax, letting out a deep breath.

"I don't know what I'm doing," he said quietly. "Mary Jane, I feel so helpless."

"But you're not helpless." He started to look away, and with her thumb she tilted his face back to her. "Look at me, Pete."

"Okay. I'm looking."

"I know you. I know who you are."

Some part of Mary Jane registered that his pupils dilated just then. Every other fiber of her being was focused on picking her words carefully, on somehow conveying everything she was feeling. "You are Peter Parker, the best person I have ever had the privilege to know. You are good and noble and strong. Your Aunt May knows that. Uncle Ben knew that."

Peter stared at her.

"And I know that if ever anything happened to anyone you loved, you would do everything in your power to save them," she continued.

Peter made the tiniest of nods.

"And if anything happened to you, the people who love you would do everything in their power to save you, too," MJ continued.

"I..." Then he paused, her words sinking in. "Do you mean that?"

She nodded, her gaze unwavering. "I trust you," she said simply. "More than anyone in the world."

He was silent for a long while, searching her features. "And I trust you."

"Good," she said. "Now you need to trust yourself." He looked startled.

"Just keep on trying," she squeezed his arm. "It's the only way anything's ever going to change. Sometimes the effort will work, sometimes it won't. But it's only when we stop trying that the effort is truly lost."

Neither of them said anything, and then slowly, Peter's lips curved into a small smile. He straightened, then grasped her hand. "Nobody in this world knows me like you do."

And she understood, without a doubt, exactly what he meant, precisely what he was talking about.

She knew.

And with that knowledge came a sudden surge inside of her, a rush of emotion that was hot and powerful and unlike anything she had ever felt in her life. It was a sense of honor that was potent and amazing and hers alone to possess.

She knew.

They stood for a long while, alone with their own thoughts and emotions, as if the rest of the universe had vanished. There was no longer any need for words.

She knew.

"Mary Jane!" Ms. Krumplesteater poked her head outside, shattering the spell. "Mary Jane," she hollered with great urgency. "Should Eliza twirl when she's dancing with the crown prince?"

"No, no twirl. More of a sweep. I'll be right there."

Finally Peter laughed. "Memo to self: sweep, don't twirl."

"Yeah, and don't you forget it, Tiger." She looked back into his wonderfully blue eyes. And once again they were bright and clear and direct.

He squeezed her hand. "You're right, MJ."

"About the twirling?"

"About the trying."

"Mary Jane!" Ms. Krumplesteater blew her whistle to get the point across.

"Later," he said. "And thank you."

There was so much she wanted to say. But instead, she simply whispered, "You're welcome."

And off he went, both realizing that whatever

indescribable thing had just transpired, only one thing was certain.

Neither would ever be the same again.

* * *

Opening night.

There was something intoxicating about the backstage bustling. The cast and crew ran about on frantic missions to put on the best show possible.

The principles were warming up their voices, with Wendy's being the loudest, clearest, and most beautiful voice of all. It had been an amazing thing to watch Wendy grow into the part of Eliza Doolittle, and to hear her singing improve week by week. The vocal coach had taken Wendy's already fine voice and honed it into something spectacular.

Her acting had gone from so-so to absolutely spellbinding. When she was onstage, it was impossible to look at anyone else. She captured the footlights and made them shine on her. Even during the few scenes she wasn't onstage, there was a clear sense of anticipation. Everyone was just biding their time until her return.

Unfortunately, that quality of time-biding was most apparent in Bernie's Professor Higgins. Unlike Wendy, his performance had wilted during the weeks of practice. What started as a lion's roar ended as an uncertain whimper. But that was fine, and actually made the chemistry work between the two. Wendy, with her powerful voice and gale-force personality was the main event, and Bernie was her weaker sidekick.

The only thing Mary Jane was really worried about were the dance numbers she had choreographed. What if they really stank? What if she had pulled a Bernie and completely messed up?

"Mary Jane, I want to show you something," said Ms. Krumplesteater backstage.

"What? Did Belinda hurt her knee again?"

"No. This." She handed her the newly printed program.

"Wow, it looks great!" She opened it up, scanning the credits. The director, the musical director, the choreographer...wait a minute. "Oh, no! It's reversed. It has me as the choreographer and you as the assistant!"

"It's not reversed," the volleyball coach said. For opening night she was resplendent in an aqua velveteen track -suit. "You did this, MJ. This would have been a complete disaster without you."

Mary Jane was speechless. "Thank you." She felt her throat tighten.

"Five minutes! Places, everyone!"

She had just time enough to do one last thing.

Wendy was pacing in the makeup area, her face smudged with black to show her in character as the poor Cockney flower girl. Around her shoulders was a torn, loosely crocheted black shawl.

"Break a leg," Mary Jane whispered.

"I think I just did. MJ, I can't do this. What was I thinking? I mean, this was all a joke, right, our trying out? Well, the prank has gone too far. It's..."

"Wendy. You will be brilliant."

"Really?" She took a deep breath. "Really?"

Mary Jane braced her shoulders. "Absolutely."

"You're not just saying that?"

"Never. After all, this is what best friends are for, isn't it?"

Wendy's eyes began to mist over, "Oh, MJ..."

"Don't you dare! You'll ruin the makeup!"

"Okay, okay!" The misty eyes became bone dry, and then the orchestra began.

They hugged once, and the show began.

* * *

What started out as enthusiastic applause grew to a deafening roar by the last scene.

Mary Jane stood backstage, watching the dancers perform brilliantly. Were they always that good?

And did her choreography always look that tight?

But above all there was Wendy, who took the show word by word, note by note, and made it into a one-woman event. Mary Jane had never seen anything like it.

"Good lord, this is incredible," shouted Mr. Toby during one of the longer bouts of applause. And it was.

If possible, Wendy seemed to feed off the audience, to grow better, stronger with every clap of approval.

And finally came the last scene, when Eliza brings the slippers to Professor Higgins, and the orchestra swells to a magical crescendo.

The end.

There was a momentary silence as the last note faded, and then the Midtown High School auditorium exploded into wild applause and shouts of "bravo!" One by one the cast took their curtain calls, and when Wendy came out the audience went absolutely crazy.

Wendy seemed more dazed than anyone else, as great armfuls of roses were handed to her or dropped at her feet.

Mary Jane was applauding as loudly as anyone else. Her hands were beginning to get sore, but she didn't care.

"Isn't this great?" She shouted to the stage manager, but he pointed to Wendy, who was motioning to her.

"Huh?" MJ mouthed.

"Come here!" Wendy called.

Mary Jane shook her head no. Wendy marched backstage, grabbed her by the wrist, cradled her bouquet in the other arm, and yanked her onstage.

There they stood, the two friends. The world itself seemed to be applauding, and as MJ's eyes adjusted to the bright footlights, she saw her mother and Captain Stacy clapping and smiling, their arms linked. A few rows away were Gwen and Harry, who was taking Gwen, Peter, and Mary Jane out to dinner after the cast party. His real friends, he said. Harry was shouting something, but she couldn't make it out. And that was probably just as well.

Front and center, grinning broadly, was Peter Parker. And as he applauded, his eyes were focused on Mary Jane. Only Mary Jane.

Wendy put her arm around her best friend and slipped a half dozen roses into her grasp. At that moment, for once, everything made perfect sense to Mary Jane Watson.

In a world gone slightly insane, in a place of noise and chaos, as long as you had people you loved, there would always be enough roses for everyone.

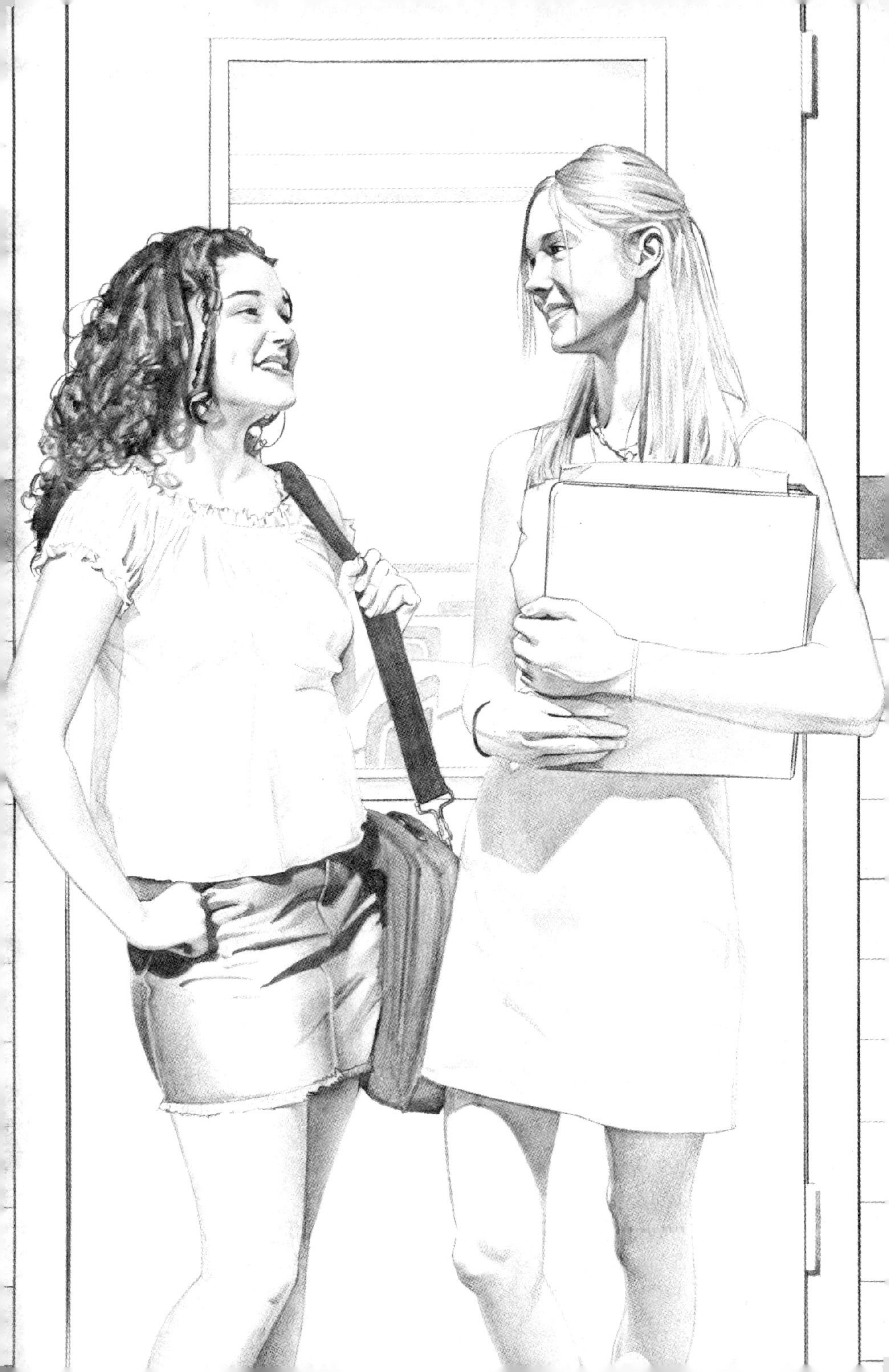